3-Point Academic Writing

**Organization,
Content,
Language**

Akiko Miyama
Mitsuko Yukishige
Tomoko Onabe
Junko Murao
Ashley Moore

KINSEIDO

Kinseido Publishing Co., Ltd.
3-21 Kanda Jimbo-cho, Chiyoda-ku,
Tokyo 101-0051, Japan
Copyright © 2019 by　Akiko Miyama
　　　　　　　　　　Mitsuko Yukishige
　　　　　　　　　　Tomoko Onabe
　　　　　　　　　　Junko Murao
　　　　　　　　　　Ashley Moore

All rights reserved. No part of this publication may be reproduced, stored in a retrieval system, or transmitted, in any form or by any means, electronic, mechanical, photocopying, recording or otherwise, without the prior permission of the publisher.

First published 2019 by Kinseido Publishing Co., Ltd.

Cover design　　parastyle inc.
Text design　　 C-leps Co., Ltd.

謝辞
本書の作成にあたり、以下の皆様に多大なるご協力をいただきました。
心より感謝の意を表します。

　　大阪工業大学　空間デザイン学科　赤井愛先生
　　大阪工業大学　システムデザイン工学科　小林裕之先生
　　大阪工業大学　空間デザイン学科卒業生　阿部光太郎氏
　　社会福祉法人　兵庫盲導犬協会施設長　田上貴久美氏

はじめに

本書では、Organization（文の構成）、Language（言語表現スタイル）、Content（伝達する内容）の3つの視点を柱とし、大学・大学院で課される授業レポート、小論文、論文、研究発表原稿などのジャンルの特徴を理解し学術文書を作成する、アカデミック・ライティングというスキル習得を目指します。アカデミック・ライティングは文書のジャンルごとに特徴的な構成やスタイルが採用され、それぞれルールは異なります。本書で扱うジャンルは、**エッセイ**、**論文のアブストラクト**、**研究発表スライドとそのスクリプト**の4種類です。

エッセイには、自由な形式で気軽に自分の意見などを述べた随筆のようなものがありますが、本書で扱うのは、意見を述べ、それを論理的にサポートしていくというスタイルの**アカデミック・エッセイ**です。アカデミック・エッセイの中にも、事象のプロセスを説明したり、問題点に対するとらえ方を論じたり分析したり、そこから導き出される解決法を示したりするなど様々なスタイルがあります。本書で取り上げたトピックは『ベジタリアン・ダイエット』と『ソーシャル・ネットワーキング・サービス』ですが、ここで学習する基本構成やスタイルはほとんどの**アカデミック・エッセイ**に応用可能です。

次に**論文のアブストラクト**ですが、**アブストラクト**とは、論文の冒頭に付けられる論文の概略のことです。題名と**アブストラクト**だけで独立して論文の検索結果に表示されることもあり、忙しい読者は題名をみて、次に**アブストラクト**を読み、そこで論文を読むのをやめてしまう場合もあるかも知れません。したがって論文の重要な情報が過不足無く書かれ、かつ読者の興味をひくように書かれていなければなりません。本書では、『ロボット亀』に関する**実験論文**を例に、**アブストラクト**の標準スタイルを学びます。

最後に『盲導犬ハーネスバッグのデザイン』をテーマにして、プレゼンテーション用**研究スライド**と**発表スクリプト**のスタイルや構成を学びます。**研究スライド**は、1ページのスライドのスペースが限られていることから、情報を簡潔に、かつ的確に伝えなければならず、独特の表現スタイルをとります。**スクリプト**は口語表現になりますが、やはりアカデミック・プレゼンテーション特有の表現ルールがあります。

本書では、ライティングの語句や文章を十分に吟味して練りなおす推敲のスキルや、徹底的に客観的に文章を読み、間違いを見つける校正のスキルも同時に学習しますので、実際に書いてみることにも挑戦してください。**研究スライド**と**発表スクリプト**を使って実際にプレゼンテーションをするのも良いでしょう。

最後になりましたが、テキスト作成の際にお世話になりました金星堂編集部の皆様に心からお礼を申し上げます。

著者

3-Point Academic Writing:
Organization, Content, Language

Table of Contents

Essay

Unit 1	Key Features of Academic Essay ▶ エッセイの重要な特徴	1
Unit 2	Title of Your Essay ▶タイトルの決定	6
Unit 3	Introduction of Your Essay ▶ イントロダクションの役割	11
Unit 4	Body of Your Essay ▶ ボディの構造	16
Unit 5	Conclusion of Your Essay ▶ コンクルージョンのまとめ方	21
Unit 6	Feedback from Others ▶ フィードバックに挑戦	26
Unit 7	Submitting Your Final Draft ▶ エッセイの最終原稿提出	31

Abstract for Research Paper

Unit 8	Structure of a Research Paper ▶ リサーチ・ペーパーの構造とイントロダクション	36
Unit 9	Key Concepts of an Abstract ▶ アブストラクトの重要な特徴	41
Unit 10	First Draft of Your Abstract ▶ アブストラクトの草稿	46
Unit 11	Rewriting Your Abstract ▶ アブストラクトの最終原稿を仕上げる	51

Presentation and Slide

Unit 12	Key Concepts of Presentations ▶ プレゼンテーションの基本的特徴	56
Unit 13	Preparing Visual Aids ▶ 視覚資料の作成	61
Unit 14	Finishing Your Scripts ▶ 発表原稿の完成	66
Unit 15	Evaluating Your Presentation ▶ プレゼンテーションの評価	71

巻末資料 ……………………………………………………… 77
- Signal Expressions for Academic Writing
- Check List
- Presentation Rubric

Unit 1

Key Features of Academic Essay

▶ エッセイの重要な特徴

Warm-up Reading

There are a variety of academic writing styles such as essays and research papers. Each form of academic writing has its own structure and written practices. Features of academic writing include organization, language, and content. First, you must have ideas and information which you want to communicate. Then you arrange the ideas or information in a logical order. When writing an essay, for example, the paragraphs should be well-linked. Finally it must be written in a formal academic style with accurate grammar and appropriate vocabulary.

☑ Comprehension Check

Warm-up Reading の英文を読み、質問に答えましょう。

1. academic writing（アカデミック・ライティング）と思われるものをすべて選びましょう。

☐ Essay ☐ Experimental report
☐ Tweet ☐ Novel
☐ Advertising leaflet ☐ Research paper

2. academic writing として不適切なルールを１つ選びましょう。

☐ Using colloquial language or slang
☐ Writing in complete sentences
☐ Writing as concisely as you can
☐ Avoiding vague words and phrases
☐ Making your writing easy to follow

3. academic writing の重要な特徴を表す英単語を３つ挙げましょう。

_____   _____   _____

Put It into Practice

▶ Organization

essay を書く場合、筋が通った論理構成にする必要があります。最初の paragraph（段落）は introduction（序論）と呼ばれ、まず essay がどのような topic（主題）で書かれているのか読者に理解させる役割を持っています。

introduction の構成
・background（背景説明）
・thesis statement（筆者の主張）
・outline（概要：どう論じるかの説明）

次の英文は、title（表題）が "Are vegetarian diets good for us?" という essay の introduction の一部を順不同に並べ替えたものです。A 〜 C を論理的な流れに並べ替えましょう。（なお、一部語法の間違いが含まれています。）

[   ] → [   ] → [   ]

A This essay argues that, with thorough planning, cut out meat from your diet can have a positive effect on your health. I will put forward three possible health benefits before discussing some of the ways in which a poorly planned vegetarian diet might not be so healthy.

B Before decide to turn vegetarian it is important to consider both the advantages and possible disadvantage of such a move. In this essay I will focus on the health implications associated with a vegetarian diet.

C The idea that people should switch to a vegetarian diet is becoming increasingly common. Proponents argues that a vegetarian diet is more ethical, better for your health and kinder to the environment.

▶▶ Language

> essayの構成がしっかりしていても、言語のスタイルがフォーマルでなかったり、語法が間違っていたりすると情報が的確に伝わりません。言語表現に細心の注意を払って書く必要があります。

以下は、Organizationのセクションで取り上げた英文を、論理の流れを考慮して並べ替えた後のものです。ここでは、語法の間違いに注目します。以下のヒントを参照しながら、1〜5の空所に適当な表現を書き入れましょう。

1. 主語と動詞を呼応させる
2. 前置詞の後ろの動詞の形を整える
3. 前後の文をスムーズにつなげるための副詞を入れる
4. 数を合わせる
5. 文の主語になるように動詞の形を整える

　　The idea that people should switch to a vegetarian diet is becoming increasingly common. Proponents ¹·argues → ＿＿＿＿ that a vegetarian diet is more ethical, better for your health and kinder to the environment. Before ²·decide → ＿＿＿＿ to turn vegetarian, ³·＿＿＿＿, it is important to consider both the advantages and possible ⁴·disadvantage → ＿＿＿＿ of such a move. In this essay I will focus on the health implications associated with a vegetarian diet. This essay argues that, with thorough planning, ⁵·cut → ＿＿＿＿ out meat from your diet can have a positive effect on your health. I will put forward three possible health benefits before discussing some of the ways in which a poorly planned vegetarian diet might not be so healthy.

▶▶▶ Content

> essayは、いきなり書き始めるのではなく前もって書く内容について考えを整理しなければなりません。代表的な思考整理法にtable（表）、bullet points（箇条書き）、mind map（マインド・マップ）があります。

1. 以下は、tableを使って思考を整理した例です。この例を参考にして、思考を整理するのにtableが適しているのはa～cのどれか答えましょう。

   Business communication tools:

In the past	Nowadays
Letter	Email, voice mail
Face-to-face meeting	Video conference
Paper document	Online document
Fixed telephone	Mobile phone

   a. 複数のアイディアの要点を整理する
   b. 比較がテーマとなっている話題を整理する
   c. 出来事を時系列に従って整理する

2. 以下は、bullet pointsを使って思考を整理した例です。ここで挙げられていない「海外留学の理由」はa～cのどれか答えましょう。

   > Reasons for studying abroad:
   > - To learn a new language
   > - To understand different cultures
   >   - To gain an attitude of openness
   >   - To broaden your perspectives
   > - To experience life in other countries
   >   - To cultivate your ability to live independently

   a. 学位を取得する
   b. 視野を広げる
   c. 語学力を身につける

3. 以下は、mind map を使って思考を整理した例です。どのような思考整理法なのかを考え、mind map を利用するのが適当でないものは a～c のどれか答えましょう。

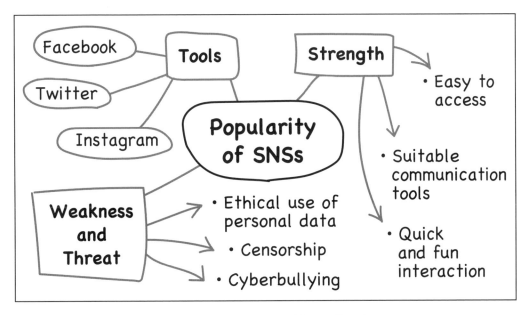

a. 2つのアイディアについて、長所・短所を比較して整理する
b. ブレーンストーミングの結果を整理する
c. アンケートの自由記述項目の回答内容を整理する

Do It Yourself

以下は、本章で取り上げた essay "Are vegetarian diets good for us?" の introduction の段落冒頭部分を、bullet points を用いて整理したものです。空所内に適当な語を書き入れ、アイディアを整理してみましょう。

- People are ^{1.}_____ to a vegetarian diet
- Proponents' argument for a vegetarian diet
  - ^{2.}_____ ethical
  - ^{3.}_____ for your health
  - ^{4.}_____ to the environment
  - Importance of ^{5.}_____ both merits and demerits
- This essay will focus on
  - possible effects on ^{6.}_____
    e.g. Cutting out meat

Unit 2

Title of Your Essay

▶ タイトルの決定

📖 Warm-up Reading

A good title is accurate, concise, and informative on the main topic of the essay, often with words to catch reader's attention. Make sure that the title is not personal. You should always capitalize the first letter of the title, but should not use a period at the end of the title, though you may use a question mark or an exclamation point. Other rules vary, but titles of academic essay usually have three parts: a catchy hook, topic keywords, and words to limit the topic.

☑ Comprehension Check

Warm-up Reading の英文を読み、質問に答えましょう。

1. 良い title の特徴として挙げられているものをすべて選びましょう。

☐ Attractive to the readers
☐ Characteristic of your personality
☐ As short as possible
☐ Concise and accurate

2. 英文から判断して、以下のtitleの中から適切でないものをすべて選びましょう。また、その理由についても考えましょう。

☐ Why I am interested in studying horsemanship
☐ Why People Choose to Live in the Suburbs
☐ Do SNSs have a negative effect on our personal relations?
☐ how to use iPads for autonomous learning.

Put It into Practice

▶Organization

> 🖉 titleの中にtopicに関する適切なkeyword（キーワード）を入れることで、そのessayのtopicが明確になります。
> titleの構造は大きく分けて、以下の3つのパートからできています。
> ① 目を引く表現
> ② topic keyword
> ③ topicを限定する語

あなたは"How important early English education is for young children"というtopicでessayを書こうとし、これまでに3回に分けてtitleを改善してきました。3回目の最終案の下線部は、それぞれ上記の説明の①〜③のどのパートにあたるか、考えて答えましょう。

1回目：Early English Education in Japan
2回目：Early English Education for Elementary School Children in Japan
3回目：
　　<u>A Necessary Tool</u>: <u>Early English Education</u> <u>for Elementary School Children in Japan</u>
　　　　[　　]　　　　　　　[　　]　　　　　　　　　　[　　]

▶▶ Language

essayのtitleの代表的な書き方には、以下のようなものがあります。
① すべての単語の頭文字を大文字で始める
　ただし、冠詞・4文字以下の前置詞・and, but などの等位接続詞・不定詞のto は小文字
② 最初の単語の頭文字のみ大文字で始め、以降はすべて固有名詞を除いて小文字にする

すでに学んだ以下の2点も忘れないようにしましょう。
・ピリオドは付けない
・topic keyword を含める

よりフォーマルな essay では、collocation や topic keyword が以下の機能を持ちます。
・collocation（連語：単語同士の自然な組み合わせ）→ essay の目的を示す
・topic keyword → 方法、場所などの具体的な情報を絞り込む

1. 上記①②に従って、以下の title を修正しましょう。

　a. Theories in second language acquisition.

　_____

　b. time And Methods of fertilizer Application

　_____

2. 以下の title の topic keyword に下線を引きましょう。

　a. Health care costs climb with weight gain

　b. The Japanese Way of Thinking: The Spirit of "Wa"

3. 以下の title の下線が引かれた collocation から、その essay の目的を推察してみましょう。

　a. <u>Analysis of</u> Gender Bias in Modern Languages

　_____

　b. <u>Characterization of</u> heroines in 19th century English novels

　_____

　c. <u>Development of</u> New Super-Speed Camera System for Single-Molecule Imaging

　_____

▶▶▶ Content

> 良いtitleとはessayの内容を的確に示すとともに、多くの読者の興味をひきつけるものです。
> ① subject（何について書くのか）
> ② purpose（何の目的で書くのか）
> ③ audience（= readers：誰を対象に書くのか）
>
> を意識して書くことは、academic writingの基本です。

1. 以下のtitleは、どちらが読者にとってより興味をひきつけられるものになっているか、考えて答えましょう。

   a. Why I Need to Sleep a Long Time Every Day
   b. The New Theory about Why Animals Sleep: To Maintain the Immune System

2. 以下は、Warm-up Readingの設問2で確認したtitleです。上記の①〜③を意識して、読者の興味をひくものに書き変えましょう。

   a. Why I am interested in studying horsemanship

   _____

   b. How to use iPads for autonomous learning

   _____

✎ Do It Yourself

以下は、Unit 1で取り上げたessay "Are vegetarian diets good for us?" のintroductionの日本語要約文と、タイトル作成の過程を例示したものです。

> 食習慣を見直すため、ベジタリアンに転向する人たちが増えている。しかし、ベジタリアンになることの長所・短所の両方をよく考慮することが大切である。このessayは、肉類を制限するダイエット法は健康に良い効果があることを論じるものである。
> **Topic keywords:** diet, vegetarian

① まず、Topic keywordsを使ってtitleの形にします。
   Vegetarian Diet is increasingly common
② 次に、論旨の展開を考え、より客観的な視点を加えます。
   Merits and Demerits of Vegetarian Diets
③ 最後に、読者に問いかけるなど、さらに魅力的にする工夫をします。
   Are Vegetarian Diets Good for Us?

前ページの例を参考にして、以下のintroductionの日本語要約文に、適切なtitleを考えてみましょう。

1.

> インターネットの発達によって現代社会が受ける恩恵はあまりにも大きい。さらにSNSは、現代人にとってなくてはならないコミュニケーションのツールであり余暇の一つとなっている。しかしながら、SNSの使用には危険もはらんでいることに我々は気づくべきであろう。SNSの功罪、特に若者にどのような影響を与えるかを論じる。
>
> **Topic keywords:** SNSs (Social Networking Services), young people

① Topic keywords を title の形に

　　SNSs are beneficial for _____ _____

② 論旨の展開を考え、より客観的に

　　Bad _____ of SNSs on _____ _____

③ さらに魅力的に→疑問文にする

　　_____ SNSs have _____ _____ on young people?

2.

> テレビ番組の多くはバラエティショー番組であり、人々の人気もあり視聴率も高い。一方で、事実を伝える報道番組や音楽、映画、時代劇などと比較すると、そのコミカルな内容の薄さからか、バラエティショー番組への批判がよく聞かれる。しかし、ニュースや芸術と共に、「笑い」は生活に不可欠なものではないだろうか。
>
> **Topic keywords:** comedy shows, entertainment, criticism

① Topic keywords を title の形に

　　Comedy shows are loved by _____

② 論旨の展開を考え、より客観的に

　　_____ against comedy shows as an _____

③ さらに魅力的に→コロン（：）と感嘆符を使う

　　Comedy Shows: an Essencial _____ in Our _____ _____ !

Unit 3

Introduction of Your Essay

▶ イントロダクションの役割

Warm-up Reading

The "introduction" is the very first paragraph of the essay, so it should capture the readers' interest, introduce the background information of the topic, state your thesis statement, and outline your essay. Usually, it starts with the general background of the topic or the reason why you chose it, then narrows to your thesis statement, and finally describes what the essay will cover. To make the flow clearer, set phrases are frequently used as signal expressions. In the "introduction" you often use the present, present continuous, present perfect or future tenses.

☑ Comprehension Check

Warm-up Reading の英文を読み、質問に答えましょう。

1. introduction に含める内容として述べられているものをすべて選びましょう。

☐ Information from books you will refer to ☐ Thesis statement
☐ General background to the topic ☐ Outline of the essay
☐ Precise and detailed description of the theme

2.「essayの論の流れを明確にするために使われるもの」として述べられているものを、1つ選びましょう。

☐ Linking verbs
☐ Background statement
☐ Signal expressions
☐ Thesis statement

3. introductionでしばしば使用される時制について述べられているものを、すべて選びましょう。

☐ 現在形／現在進行形／現在完了形
☐ 過去完了形
☐ 過去形／過去進行形
☐ 未来形

Put It into Practice

▶ Organization

introductionでは、essayのbackgroundやthesis statement、またoutlineを明らかにする必要があります。一般的(general)な背景情報を述べることから始め、次第に自分が主張したい内容に特化(specific)して情報を絞り込んでいくように、いわば「逆三角形の構造」にしましょう。

essayのintroductionでは、background、thesis statement、outlineは、それぞれ以下の「逆三角形の構造」のどの場所に来るべきでしょうか。考えて書き入れましょう。

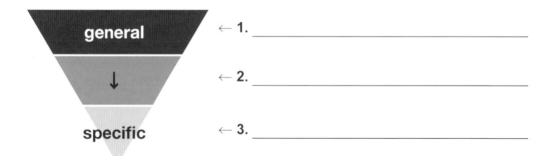

▶▶ Language

 introductionでは、以下のようなsignal expressions（合図表現）がよく使われます。
・topicの背景情報を紹介するための事実やデータ、引用を導入する表現
・essayの流れを説明する表現
また、疑問文を使用して読者の興味を喚起することも、有効な表現方法です。

以下は、Unit 1で取り上げたessay "Are vegetarian diets good for us?" のintroductionです。

The idea that people should switch to a vegetarian diet is becoming increasingly common. Proponents argue that a vegetarian diet is more ethical, better for your health and kinder to the environment. Before deciding to turn vegetarian, however, it is important to consider both the advantages and possible disadvantages of such a move. In this essay I will focus on the health implications associated with a vegetarian diet. This essay argues that, with thorough planning, cutting out meat from your diet can have a positive effect on your health. I will put forward three possible health benefits before discussing some of the ways in which a poorly planned vegetarian diet might not be so healthy.

1. 使われている時制は何でしょうか。 _____

2. 論の流れをより明確にするために使われていると考えられるsignal expressionsを探し、できる限り抜き出しましょう。

_____   _____
_____   _____
_____

3. 上記のintroductionを参考に、a〜eのsignal expressionsは、background [BG]、thesis statement [TS]、outline [OL] のどこで使用されるのか、答えましょう。

    a. This essay examines ...　　[　　]
    b. I will explore ...　　[　　]
    c. Generally, ...　　[　　]
    d. In recent years, ...　　[　　]
    e. I will put forward ...　　[　　]

▶▶▶ Content

> backgroundを提示する時は、事実や簡単なデータを示しますが、読者の興味をひくためには逸話や引用などを入れるのも良いでしょう。

Languageのセクションで読んだintroductionには、読者の興味をひくための事実やデータを示す一文が含まれています。もう一度introductionに目を通し、その一文の最初の２語を書き出しましょう。

_____   _____

Do It Yourself

同じフォーマットを使って、「原子力使用反対」あるいは「持続可能なエネルギーの使用促進」に関するessayのintroductionを書いてみましょう。選択肢の語句を空所に書き入れ、introductionのbackground、thesis statement、outlineを作ります。なお、同じアルファベットの空所には同じ語句が入ります。

1. 原子力使用反対

background	The idea that people should a. _____ b. _____ is becoming increasingly common. Before deciding to do it, however, it is important to consider both the c. _____ and possible disadvantages of such a move.
thesis statement	The essay argues that b. _____ can d. _____ on the earth.
outline	I will put forward some possible disadvantages before discussing c. _____ of b. _____.

```
        have a devastating effect      get rid of
                advantages     nuclear power
```

2. 持続可能なエネルギーの使用促進

background	The idea that people should ᵉ·_____ ᶠ·_____ is becoming increasingly common. Before deciding to do it, however, it is important to consider both the ᵍ·_____ and possible disadvantages of such a move.
thesis statement	The essay argues that ᶠ·_____ can ʰ·_____ on the earth.
outline	I will put forward some possible disadvantages before discussing ᵍ·_____ of ᶠ·_____.

> sustainable energy　　advantages
> turn to　　bring environmental benefits

Unit 4

Body of Your Essay

▶ ボディの構造

📖 Warm-up Reading

　The "body" provides paragraphs with more details such as facts, examples and evidence to support the thesis statement shown in the "introduction." Each paragraph has a single main idea, which is in the topic sentence often located at the beginning of the paragraph. A topic sentence is followed by supporting sentences to add more details. The paragraphs in the essay are connected logically with conjunctions or signal expressions as discourse markers.

　The informative essay has several formats such as topic-based, time order, spatial arrangement, cause & effect, and procedural. The persuasive essay also has problem-solving and comparative advantage formats, etc.

☑ Comprehension Check

Warm-up Reading の英文を読み、質問に答えましょう。

1. body の paragraph に含めるべき内容をすべて選びましょう。

☐ Literature quoted
☐ Facts to support the thesis statement

☐ Purpose of the essay
☐ Conjunctions to connect paragraphs
☐ Related evidence

2. essayの2つのtypeを挙げましょう。

　　a. _____　　b. _____

3. 設問2で解答した2つのtypeには、いくつかのformatがあると述べられています。それらをすべて書き出しましょう。

　　a. _____

　　b. _____

Put It into Practice

▶ Organization

essayは、introduction → body → conclusion の流れで構成されます。bodyの各paragraphでは、introductionで提示されたthesis statementを支える理由や例などが述べられます。まず始めに述べたい内容（main idea）を含む主題文（topic sentence）があり、その後で、理由や例などを説明する文章（supporting sentences）が続きます。1つのparagraphに入るmain ideaは1つだけです。

以下の図は、5つのparagraphsから成る1つのessayの構造を表したものです。paragraph 1〜5が、introduction、body、conclusionのどれにあたるか考え、下図の下線部に書き入れましょう。

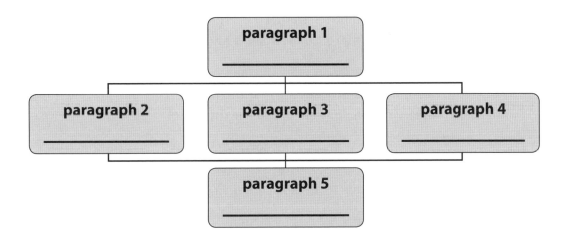

▶▶ Language

> 各paragraphは、それぞれ論理的な流れで繋がっていなければなりません。そのためには、論理の繋がりや移り変わりを示すsignal expressionsが必要です。bodyの代表的なformatには、頻繁に使用される特徴的なsignal expressionsがあります。

1. 以下のsignal expressionsを、役割によってグループ分けしましょう。

| generally | in conclusion | what is more | on the contrary |
| first / second / third | for instance | as a result | likewise |

- **a.** リストアップ ＿＿＿＿＿＿＿＿
- **b.** 一般化 ＿＿＿＿＿＿＿＿
- **c.** 例示 ＿＿＿＿＿＿＿＿
- **d.** 補強 ＿＿＿＿＿＿＿＿
- **e.** 同意・同調 ＿＿＿＿＿＿＿＿
- **f.** 反意・逆接 ＿＿＿＿＿＿＿＿
- **g.** 結果 ＿＿＿＿＿＿＿＿
- **h.** 結論 ＿＿＿＿＿＿＿＿

2. 次のa〜eのsignal expressionsのグループに合わせて、それらを多用するformat名を以下の選択肢より選び、書き入れましょう。

Spatial arrangement（空間的配列）	Cause & effect（原因と結果）
Topic-based（項目別）	Procedural（作業手順）
Comparative advantage（比較的優位性）	

- **a.** ＿＿＿＿＿＿＿＿＿＿＿＿＿＿ format
  first / to begin with / second / next / then / in addition / after / before / besides / furthermore / finally

- **b.** ＿＿＿＿＿＿＿＿＿＿＿＿＿＿ format
  X differs from Y / X is more … than Y / on the other hand / in contrast to / unlike X, Y is … / one difference between X and Y is

- **c.** ＿＿＿＿＿＿＿＿＿＿＿＿＿＿ format
  in front of / behind / beside / next to / on the left of / between / on the top of / opposite / across / at the bottom of / in the middle of

- **d.** ＿＿＿＿＿＿＿＿＿＿＿＿＿＿ format
  X causes Y / Because of Y / due to X / X is attributable to Y / X is responsible for Y / X leads to Y / X results in Y / therefore

- **e.** ＿＿＿＿＿＿＿＿＿＿＿＿＿＿ format
  X consists of Y / X is characterized by Y / X features Y / X is composed of Y

▶▶▶ Content

> bodyの各paragraphでは、topic sentenceにおいて、introductionで示したthesis statementの「主張を支える理由」を述べるのが一般的です。topic sentenceに続くsupporting sentencesでは、それらの主張をさらに具体的に説明します。keywordsを各paragraphに入れると、主題を常に印象づけられます。

以下は、essay "Are vegetarian diets good for us?" のbodyです。

A Evidence suggests that one possible benefit of a vegetarian diet is a lower risk of becoming obese. A study published in 2013 in the journal of the Academy of Nutrition and Dietetics found that even though the number of calories consumed by vegetarians in the study was about the same as that of meat-eaters, the vegetarians had a lower average body mass index (BMI). As most people are now aware, obesity is linked to a range of health problems and has been proven to lower an individual's life expectancy. This evidence suggests that avoiding meat could lead to a longer, healthier life.

B According to the American Heart Association, eating your greens can also be a smart choice for your heart, too. The association's website points out that vegetarians have a lower risk of suffering from high blood pressure and coronary heart disease. Together, these lowered dangers also result in a lower risk of suffering from a potentially fatal heart attack. While the association is careful to emphasize the need for a planned diet (a point discussed further below), the benefits for one's health seem to be clear.

C The last health benefit I shall discuss is based on limited evidence that a vegetarian diet can lead to a lower incidence of some forms of cancer. According to the Harvard Medical School, because vegetarian diets obviously do not include red meat, vegetarians are less likely to suffer from colon cancer. Although this could be said for all diets that avoid red meats (not just vegetarianism), we can say that this is an added benefit of sticking to a plant-only regime.

D However, as noted earlier, most official advice on adopting a vegetarian diet stresses the need for people to plan their changes carefully in order to make sure they are not missing out on vital nutrients their bodies need such as protein, calcium, and vitamins B12 and D. In addition, not all "vegetarian" foods are necessarily healthy. It is quite possible to obtain most of our calories from snack foods like soda and pizza and still technically not be eating any meat. In this case it is unlikely that you will actually be enjoying many health benefits.

1. paragraph A〜Dのtopic sentenceに下線を引き、supporting sentencesについてはtopic sentenceに対する役割を確認しましょう。

2. introductionで示されたthesis statementのkeywordsを、各paragraphから探して○で囲みましょう。

✏️ Do It Yourself

1. 以下のformatの空所a～cに、選択肢の語を書き入れましょう。

| Differences | solutions | Disadvantages |

賛成・反対／長所・短所／比較・対照

Introduction		Background, Thesis Statement
Body	Paragraph 1	* Why you agree / Advantages / Similarities
	Paragraph 2	* Why you disagree / a._____ / b._____
	Paragraph 3	* Discussions
Conclusion		Summary of main ideas, Proposal, Prediction

原因と結果や問題と解決

Introduction		Background, Thesis Statement
Body	Paragraph 1	* The most important reason / cause 1 for problem
	Paragraph 2	* The less important reason / cause 2 for problem
	Paragraph 3	* Offer some c._____
Conclusion		Summary of main ideas, Proposal, Prediction

2. Contentのセクションで読んだbodyの各paragraphから、signal expressionsを書き出しましょう。次に、signal expressionsがparagraphの中でどのような役割を果たしているか、考えてみましょう。

A. _____

B. _____

C. _____

D. _____

Unit 5

Conclusion of Your Essay

▶ コンクルージョンのまとめ方

📖 Warm-up Reading

The "conclusion" is not the place to present important new facts or references. This paragraph usually includes a restatement of the thesis, brief summary of the main ideas, and the final statement to leave something for the reader to think about. It is a good idea to start the paragraph with a signal expression such as "To conclude," "In summary," or "In conclusion," then rephrase the thesis statement mentioned in the introduction. After the brief summary, you could also ask questions, offer some solutions, recommendations, and predictions to the reader.

☑ Comprehension Check

Warm-up Readingの英文を読み、質問に答えましょう。

1. 英文によると、conclusionはいくつの部分に分けられますか。

_____

2. conclusionに含める内容をすべて選びましょう。

☐ Rephrased thesis statement from the introduction
☐ Examples of the statement mentioned earlier
☐ Summary of the literature quoted
☐ Summary of the main ideas in each paragraph

3. conclusionに含めるべきでない内容をすべて選びましょう。

☐ New ideas unstated in the previous paragraphs
☐ Solution to the topic problem
☐ Future trends
☐ References to previously unmentioned sources

Put It into Practice

▶ Organization

 conclusionは、以下のような構造で進みます。
・始めに、introductionで示した主題を言い換えた表現で繰り返す：restatement
・次に、bodyの各paragraphのmain ideasをまとめる：summary
・最後に、今後の予測や展望、提案、解決策、主張の限界などを述べる：final statement

　introductionは一般的な情報から特化した内容に絞り込んでいく「逆三角形の構造」でしたが、conclusionは、特化されたthesis statementからより大きな課題へと一般化していく「三角形の構造」で、specificな内容から次第にgeneralな情報へ拡大していきます。

1. conclusionでは、以下の選択肢の項目は「三角形の構造」のどの場所に来るべきでしょうか。

　　将来の展望、提案、課題 / 各paragraphの要約 / introductionでの主題の言い換え

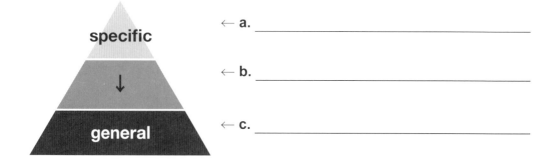

2. 以下はessay "Are vegetarian diets good for us?" のconclusionのparagraphを順不同に並べ替えたものです。どのparagraphがrestatement、summary、final statementに当たるかを考えて空所に書き入れ、A～Cを論理的な流れに並べ替えましょう。

[　　]→[　　]→[　　]

A [＿＿＿＿＿＿＿＿＿＿＿] Take the time to consider your own diet and lifestyle. Your body may thank you for it in the long run.

B [＿＿＿＿＿＿＿＿＿＿＿] Obesity, heart attacks, and cancer are some of the leading causes of death in modern society, but becoming vegetarian can lower your risk factors.

C [＿＿＿＿＿＿＿＿＿＿＿] In conclusion, although it is important to conscientiously plan one's switch to vegetarianism, the official advice suggests that doing so can have important health advantages for most people.

▶▶ Language

conclusionでの主張は、essay内で前述したparagraphのmain ideasの根拠に基づいた議論です。そのため、単文 (simple sentence) よりは、物事の理由や結論・結果を表す従位接続詞 (though, since, etc.) で繋がった複文 (complex sentence) になることが多くなります。

例　As I mentioned above, X is ...　The evidence suggests that ...,
　　Although it is important to ...,　We also need ...

1. 上記の説明の例を参考にして、2つの単文を従位接続詞で繋いで1つの複文にしましょう。

It is important to conscientiously plan one's switch to vegetarianism.
＋ But the official advice suggests that doing so can have important health advantages.

_____
_____

2. 以下のsignal expressionsを、役割に合わせて選びましょう。

| in summary | further studies are needed | to conclude |

a　今からconclusionを述べる　　　　　_____
b．これまでの内容を要約する　　　　　_____
c．conclusionの限界や今後の展望を述べる　_____

▶▶▶ Content

> conclusionで、各paragraphを要約しintroductionのthesis statementを繰り返す際には、同じ語句で表現するのではなく、別の表現を使用して書き換え（paraphrase）ましょう。また、提案や今後の展望を述べ、疑問文を含めるなど、読者に考えを促すようにすると良いでしょう。

1. 以下は別の表現を使って書き換える方法です。a～gの空所に選択肢の語を書き入れましょう。

| the number of ~ is increasing | greens | be beneficial |
| make a presentation | good idea | discuss | according to a data |

同義語・類義語・代名詞で書き換え

now	recently	people	we
argue	a. [ ]	stress	emphasize
essay	paper	incident	occurrence / event
smart choice	b. [ ]	miss out	lack in
vegetables	c. [ ]	according to A	A says
cut out meat	stop eating meat		
evidence suggests that	d. [ ]		
have a positive effect	e. [ ]		

品詞を換えて書き換え

benefit (v.)	beneficial (adj.) benefits (n.)
present (v.)	f. [ ] (n.)

文の構成を換えて書き換え

more and more ~	g. [ ]
... before discussing that	... then, discuss that
A can lead to B	B can be caused by A
In this study, ~ is the main topic	This study discusses ~

2. 以下の英文を、指示に従って書き換えましょう。なお、同じアルファベットの空所には同じ語句が入ります。

People can benefit more from a vegetarian diet than a meat-eating one.

ステップ1：主語を1人称代名詞に
→ a._____ can benefit more from a vegetarian diet than a meat-eating one.

ステップ2：動詞 benefit を名詞 benefits に
→ There b._____ for us on a vegetarian diet than a meat-eating one.

ステップ3：benefit を形容詞に
→ A vegetarian diet is c._____ for us than a meat-eating one.
→ It is c._____ for us to have a vegetarian diet than a meat-eating one.

✎ Do It Yourself

essay "Are vegetarian diets good for us?" の introduction の thesis statement を別の表現で表し、各 paragraph の主題文の main idea を簡潔にまとめ、conclusion を作成しましょう。

Introduction		This essay argues that cutting out meat from your diet can have a positive effect on your health before discussing how a poorly planned vegetarian diet might not be so healthy.
Body	P 1	Evidence suggests that one possible benefit of a vegetarian diet is a lower risk of becoming obese.
	P 2	According to the American Heart Association, eating your greens can also be a smart choice for your heart, too.
	P 3	The last health benefit I shall discuss is based on limited evidence that a vegetarian diet can lead to a lower incidence of some forms of cancer.
	P 4	However, as noted earlier, most official advice on adopting a vegetarian diet stresses the need for people to plan their changes carefully in order to make sure they are not missing out on vital nutrients their bodies need.
Conclusion		In conclusion, although eating less a._____ is beneficial for us, we need to carefully plan the b._____ diet. According to a doctor, vegetables have good c._____ on our heart and lead to a lower risk of cancer. d._____, we should consider our diet not to miss out sufficient e._____.

Unit 6

Feedback from Others

▶フィードバックに挑戦

📖 Warm-up Reading

In this unit, the draft of your essay might be examined by your teacher or fellow students before submitting it. This procedure is called "peer review." They will provide feedback for you to consider when making amendments to your essay and help you finish up your final draft. The reviewers will give their feedback on the three aspects that you should consider when writing: such as organization, language and contents. This process is also very important in terms of improving your draft by yourself.

☑ Comprehension Check

Warm-up Reading の英文を読み、質問に答えましょう。

1. peer review（ピア・レビュー：査読）の例として適当なものをすべて選びましょう。

☐ 同じ分野を研究している学生同士のエッセイの評価
☐ 研究チーム内の同僚研究者による当該実験レポートの内容吟味
☐ 自分自身で行う論文内容の推敲
☐ 同領域の専門家たちによる論文の原稿のチェック
☐ 出版社の編集者による校正作業

2. peer reviewの際、どのような点に着目して修正ポイントを指摘すると良いでしょうか。日本語で３点挙げましょう。

_____ _____ _____

✏ Put It into Practice

▶ Organization

🖉 essayのfeedback（フィードバック）作業を行う場合、まずはorganizationの適否を判断することが重要です。論の流れが悪いと、語彙・語法が間違っていなくても、読者にメッセージが正確に伝わらないことがあります。まずは、語彙・語法の訂正にこだわらず全体を流し読みをして、論の流れを確認しましょう。

1. 以下は、organizationが適合しているかどうかを判断するためのチェックリストです。a～fに当てはまる語を選択肢から選んで書き入れましょう。

solution	background	topic
thesis	main	examples

Check List

Introduction
- ☐ some general ^{a.} _____ to the topic
- ☐ ^{b.} _____ statement
- ☐ outline

Body
- ☐ clear ^{c.} _____ sentence
- ☐ supporting sentences with details and ^{d.} _____

Conclusion
- ☐ restate of thesis statement
- ☐ summarized ^{e.} _____ ideas of the paragraphs
- ☐ concluding suggestion / prediction / ^{f.} _____

2. 以下はソーシャルネットワーキングサービスについてのessayのintroductionと、bodyの冒頭のparagraphです。各paragraphの重要事項が盛り込まれているかどうかを確認するために、設問1のチェックリストに✓を入れて、足りない情報を確認しましょう。

Discuss the reasons why social networking services are so popular.

  Social networking services(SNSs) is an important feature of modern life around the world. The biggest SNS, Facebook, have over 1.5 billion global users and other services like Twitter and Instagram have also been growing in recent years. So why is these services so popular? I would argue that their popularity is the result of three factors: the fact that these services are easy to use, the suitability of the services as a way of communicating in a globarized world, and their ability to allow for quick and fun interaction between friend.

 In the early days of the internet, if you wanted to set up your own website, you would have to learn how to code. Nowadays you can log on to an SNS like Twitter and have your own webpage in a matter of minutes. All you really need is an internet connection and an email address. The business model of most SNSs also means that most services they provide to general users are completely free. This level of accessibility is clearly one of the main reasons for their success.

▶▶ Language

languageに関してpeer reviewする場合、日本人が特に間違えやすい語法（時制・数・主語と動詞の呼応）を中心にチェックをすると良いでしょう。これに加え、些細なミスのように見えるかもしれませんが、句読点やスペース、レイアウトも間違えやすい重要ポイントなので注意が必要です。

1. Organizationのセクションの設問2の英文中、波線部は、peer reviewで修正、あるいは検討を促された部分です。それぞれを適当な形に訂正しましょう。

    a. Discuss the reasons why social networking services are so popular.

    → _____

    b. Social networking services(SNSs) is → _____

    c. The biggest SNS, Facebook, have → _____

    d. So why is these services → _____

    e. globarized → _____

    f. interaction between friend → _____

2. 語法の間違いでない箇所は、指摘漏れがある場合もあります。例えば、Organization のセクションの英文では、第1段落の以下の部分は、services という単語が繰り返され、冗長になっています。適切な表現に変更しましょう。

I would argue that their popularity is the result of three factors: the fact that these services are easy to use, the suitability of the services as a way of communicating ...

_____

_____

▶▶▶ Content

🖉 peer review する essay について、Unit 1 でも学習した table や bullet points、mind map を使って「内容」を整理してみると、論の流れが良くないところが見えてきます。

Organization のセクションの英文では、introduction に続く body の冒頭 paragraph に topic sentence を加えると、論の流れがよりスムーズになります。どのような topic sentence が適当か検討するために、内容を整理しましょう。

1. introduction の構成を bullet points で整理し、分析します。空所内に適当な語句を書き入れましょう。

Introduction

Some general background to the topic
- SNS → important feature of modern life around the world
  e.g. a._____, b._____, c._____

Thesis statement
- Discuss the reasons for their popularity

Outline
- d._____ of using them
- e._____ as a way of communicating in a globalized world
- Quick and fun f._____ between friends

Unit 6 Feedback from Others

2. 以下のA〜Cは、body部分の3つのparagraphのtopic sentenceです。設問1のbullet pointsを参考にして、空所に入れる適当な表現を選択肢から選んで書き入れましょう。次に、bodyの冒頭paragraphに入れるべきtopic sentenceをA〜Cから選びましょう。

> Another reason is that　　　Firstly　　　Lastly

A: _____ , SNSs have made communication between people fast and enjoyable.

B: _____ , SNSs are popular because they are very easy for people with very little technical knowledge to use.

C: _____ the world is becoming increasingly globalized and they allow users the opportunity to communicate with people around the world, regardless of distance and time differences.

Do It Yourself

以下の英文は、本章で取り上げたSNSについてのessayのconclusionです。

　We know that SNSs are very popular and essential in our daily life. In this essay I have put forward what I think is the three main reasons for this. We should also note that growing numbers of problem are also cause some services to see slowdowns in its growth. The ethical use of personal data, censorship, and cyber-bullying are just three of the issues face SNSs and its users. Even so, it is very probable that SNSs are here to stay and will continue to evolve with our changing world.

1. 英文中には①5つの表現の間違いと、②論の流れがスムーズでないところが1箇所あります。ピア・レビューをしているつもりで、指摘して訂正しましょう。

2. conclusionの構成について、aに相当する部分に下線を、bに相当する部分に波線を引きましょう。

　a. summarized main ideas of the paragraphs
　b. concluding prediction

Unit 7

Submitting Your Final Draft

▶ エッセイの最終原稿提出

📖 Warm-up Reading

Now you will make some amendments to your first draft by reflecting on the feedback from your fellow students. If you do not have any reviewer available, you must do this checking process by yourself. Therefore, in academic writing, your final goal should be acquiring these self-checking skills. You should keep in mind another important point. Before submitting your essay, you should check it for originality. If you publish another writer's opinions or thoughts as if they are your own, it is called "plagiarism" and plagiarists will be severely penalized. Well, it is time for you to submit your final draft.

☑ Comprehension Check

Warm-up Reading の英文を読み、質問に答えましょう。

1. academic writing において身につけるべき最終目標のスキルとは何か、1つ選びましょう。

☐ 正確な peer review をしてくれる仲間を見つけるスキル
☐ 自分の著作物を独力で推敲できるスキル
☐ 過去の著作物を参考にしなくてもオリジナルなものが書ける技術

2. 以下はplagiarism（剽窃／盗用）の定義文です。（　　）内の語句を並べ替えましょう。

Plagiarism is (full acknowledgment / the copying or paraphrasing / your own work / of another writer's work or ideas / into / without).

Plagiarism is _____

_____.

Put It into Practice

▶ Organization

自分のessayをセルフチェックする場合も、まずはorganizationの適否を判断することが重要です。Unit 6で学習したチェックリストを、セルフチェックの際にも活用しましょう。

以下は、「スマートフォンの人気」についてのessayです。自分で書いたと仮定して、構成のセルフチェックを行います。（英文中の番号と下線はLanguageのセクションで使用します。）

The reasons why people like to use smartphones

　The number of smartphone users worldwide reached 2.08 billion in 2016 and a smartphone is one of the favorite handheld devices. There are several reasons for its popularity. It gives people quick and easy access to the required information using a variety of apps.

　1. Smartphone are popular because users can access the internet anytime and anywhere by 2. use them. Even though they do not have computers 3., They can get necessary information quickly and easily. Some use phones for their studies and others for work.

　For example, there 4. is apps such as iTunes that make it easier to download music, images and movies as well as games. People do not need to go to certain places to get 5. it. They can reach their destination without being lost by taking advantage of the GPS function of smartphones.

　Nowadays smartphones have become 6. esential gadgets in everyday life and people make the best use of them in various fields 7. such education, work and entertainment.

1. 以下のチェックリストを用いて、前ページのessayの構成をセルフチェックしましょう。

Check List

Introduction
- ☐ some general background to the topic
- ☐ thesis statement
- ☐ outline

Body
1st paragraph
- ☐ clear topic sentence
- ☐ supporting sentences with details and examples

2nd paragraph
- ☐ clear topic sentence
- ☐ supporting sentences with details and examples

Conclusion
- ☐ restate of thesis statement
- ☐ summarized main ideas of the paragraphs
- ☐ concluding suggestion / prediction / solution

---

2. セルフチェックの結果に基づいて、aとbの英文をそれぞれessayのどこに加えれば良いか、答えましょう。

a. They will continue to be applied to various aspects of the ubiquitous society.

_____

b. The availability of a variety of apps is another reason for their popularity.

_____

▶▶ Language

> 🖉 ワープロソフトの校正機能を用いると、動詞の呼応や時制、またつづりのミスなどの基本的なチェックを行うことができます。

Organization の essay の英文中、波線部は、文法あるいは語彙選択についてワープロで検討を促された部分です。それぞれを適当な形に訂正しましょう。

1. Smartphone are → _____
2. by use → _____
3. ,They → _____
4. there is → _____
5. to get it → _____
6. esential gadgets → _____
7. such education → _____

▶▶▶ Content

> 🖉 plagiarism（剽窃／盗用）を避けるため、自分の考えや言葉でないことを述べる際は、その出典を明らかにする必要があります。
> また一方で、実際に書き始めると「せっかく出したアイディアだから」と不必要な情報を残してしまうことがあります。必要がないアイディアは削除しながら書くよう気をつけましょう。

1. Organization のセクションの「スマートフォンの人気」についての essay には、plagiarism になりかねない部分があります。その部分に下線を引きましょう。

2. 設問1で下線を引いた情報は、新聞記事からとられていると仮定すると、ある表現を冒頭に付けることで plagiarism ではなくなります。空所に適当な語句を書き入れましょう。
   _____ a newspaper article, ...

3. この essay の中には、全体の論の流れを妨げる削除すべき一文が混ざっています。その文に下線を引き、なぜ論の流れが妨げられるのか、その理由を述べましょう。

Do It Yourself

以下は「日本人大学生の食生活」に関するessayのconclusion部分です。自分で書いたと仮定して、セルフチェックを行います。

Undergraduate students in Japan live on a relative unhealthy diet. The students make diet decisions based on convenience and cost, which usually results in make poor nutritional choices. Many are aware of the adverse effect on their health. Thus, one solution to the problem is to be provided information about methods of preparing healthier food quick and cheap. This may help those students who recognizes the need for change to hurdle cost and convenience problems, lead them to improve their dietary habits.

1. 以下のプロセスに従って、conclusionのセルフチェックを行いましょう。

Organization
Organizationのセクションのチェックリストのconclusionの部分を使って、構造が適切かどうかを確認する。

Language
文法、語彙の選択が適切かどうかを確認する。

Content
情報の過不足とplagiarismについて確認する。

2. 以下は、セルフチェックの内容に基づいて書き直したconclusionです。上記の確認事項に関する修正すべき点が、空所で示されています。適当な語句を書き入れましょう。

a._____ a government survey, undergraduate students in Japan live on a b._____ unhealthy diet. c._____ _____ make diet decisions based on convenience and cost, which usually results in d._____ poor nutritional choices. e._____ _____, many are aware of the adverse effect on their health. Thus, one solution to the problem is to f._____ information about methods of preparing healthier food g._____. This may help those students who h._____ the need for change to hurdle the cost and convenience problems, i._____ them to improve their dietary habits.

Unit 8

Structure of a Research Paper

▶ リサーチ・ペーパーの構造とイントロダクション

📖 Warm-up Reading

Research papers normally have a set format. This RP (research paper) format describes the order of the sections of academic research papers. It often includes: title, abstract, introduction, materials and methods, results and discussion, and conclusion. Sometimes results and discussion are combined into one section, or the conclusion is included in the discussion as a final concluding paragraph. In some fields, when the materials and methods section is very long, it is often placed at the end of the paper or written separately. Among these sections, the introduction is a key section to interest your audience and give an overview of what to expect in your paper. That is why the introduction may repeat some parts of the abstract, which is perfectly acceptable.

☑ Comprehension Check

Warm-up Readingの英文を読み、質問に答えましょう。

1. research paperについて、正しい選択肢を選び文章を完成させましょう。

　　a. The RP format describes the (order / language / reader) of the sections.

b. The sections that could be combined are (methods and results sections / results and discussion sections / introduction and results section).
   c. The section that may be written separately is (results section / discussion section / materials and methods section).

2. introductionはその目的が似ていることから、他のどのセクションと内容が重なる部分があると述べられていますか。また、その共通の目的とは何か、答えましょう。

重なるセクション：＿＿＿＿＿＿＿＿＿＿＿＿＿＿＿＿＿＿＿＿＿＿＿＿＿＿＿

共通の目的：＿＿＿＿＿＿＿＿＿＿＿＿＿＿＿＿＿＿＿＿＿＿＿＿＿＿＿＿＿

＿＿＿＿＿＿＿＿＿＿＿＿＿＿＿＿＿＿＿＿＿＿＿＿＿＿＿＿＿＿＿＿＿＿＿

3. RP formatには論文のresearch topic（研究トピック）の展開によって、代表的な以下の3つのorganizationがあります。空所に当てはまるものを選択肢から選びましょう。

Ver. 1: title – [　] – introduction – [　] – [　] – discussion – conclusion
Ver. 2: title – [　] – introduction – [　] – [　] & discussion – conclusion
Ver. 3: title – [　] – introduction – [　] & discussion – conclusion – [　]

a. results　　**b.** materials & methods　　**c.** abstract

Put It into Practice

▶ Organization

research paperも、essayと同様に本体はintroductionから始まりますが、RP特有の情報が含まれるのが特徴です。

RPのintroductionの構造
・background（研究の背景）
・previous study（先行研究）
・research gap（当該分野の研究が不十分な点、但し研究内容や分野によって省かれる場合もある）
・present study（自分の研究＝本研究）

1. 以下は一般的なRPのintroductionに含まれる情報です。a～dを論理的な流れに並べ替えましょう。

   c → [　] → [　] → [　]

   a. present study　　**b.** previous study　　**c.** background　　**d.** research gap

2. 以下の英文は「絶滅危惧種とされるカメgopher tortoise（アナホリガメ）に代わるロボットカメ開発」に関する論文の、introductionの冒頭部分です。設問1の「RPのintroductionに含まれる情報」a〜dのうち、述べられていないものを記号で答えましょう。

The gopher tortoise (as shown in Fig. 1) is native to the southeastern region of Crotania and is considered to be a keystone species because the burrows it creates across its habitat provide shelter from high temperatures, forest fires and predators to over 360 different species of animal [1][2].

Fig. 1 gopher tortoise

However, numbers of gopher tortoises have fallen dramatically due to loss of habitat [3], disease [4] and being killed or taken as pets by humans [5]. At present, they are considered to be a vulnerable species [6]. This decline in population and the resultant loss of gopher tortoise burrows could thus have a serious negative impact on the ecology of the tortoise's typical habitat.

3. 設問2のintroductionで [ ] で示されているように、先行研究を引用する場合は順に参考文献番号を入れ、さらに詳しい情報を論文末にリストにして掲載します。以下の内容にあたる先行研究をそれぞれ1つ、参考文献番号で答えましょう。

  a. 現在この種のカメが脆弱種だと述べている論文　　　　　　　[　　]
  b. カメの個体数激減の理由として生息地の喪失を挙げた論文　　[　　]
  c. カメの個体数激減の理由として病気を挙げた論文　　　　　[　　]

▶▶ Language

> introductionの最終目的は、自分の研究がその分野で占める位置とその重要性をアピールすることにあります。背景と先行研究の紹介によってうまく背景理解へと導いた後は、ぐっと関心を自分の研究へと向けていくよう、言葉遣いの工夫をします。

Organization のセクションで読んだ論文のintroductionの続きを使って、previous study から present study へ移行していく過程を確認しましょう。

1. 下線部では、この論文の著者たち (Catherine Berry, Pablo Ferdinand and Shizuka Nishikawa) が、過去に出版した論文 [7] も先行研究として引用しています。以下の参考文献を参照して、aとbに当てはまる語句を選択肢から選びましょう。

参考文献 [論文末に掲載されているもの]

[7] Catherine Berry, Pablo Ferdinand and Shizuka Nishikawa, *The Biomimetic Development of Digging Robots Based on a Gopher Tortoise*. (University of Crotania Press, 2017).

In 2017, ^{a.} (Berry et al. / Berry / Berry and Ferdinand) have proposed the biomimetic development of digging robots based on the gopher tortoise that can be used to maintain the necessary number of burrows across the habitat until conservation efforts to restore tortoise populations take effect. [7] ^{b.} (We / They / He) have successfully analyzed actual tortoise digging motions, identified the component movements and created a control program that can accurately mimic these movements in a simulated test.

2. 以下はpresent studyに絞り込んでいくintroductionの締めくくりの部分です。論の流れが自然になるよう、空所に当てはまる signal expression を選択肢から選び書き入れましょう。なお、文頭に来る語も小文字で示しています。

| while | in this paper | the results suggest | by comparing |

^{a.} _____ we introduce the RoboGoph prototype and validate it ^{b.} _____ its digging motion with data from actual gopher tortoise digging motions, showing a high level of replication accuracy. ^{c.} _____ further development and testing will be necessary before RoboGoph can be considered fit for practical use, ^{d.} _____ that RoboGoph could provide a real temporary solution to the current population problem.

▶▶▶ Content

> introductionの内容の巧拙は、情報をいかに上手く並べるかで決まります。一般的背景から、過不足なく情報を入れつつトピックを絞り込み、自分の研究の重要性をアピールできるよう内容を吟味しましょう。

本章で取り上げた「ロボットカメの開発」の論文のintroductionにおいて、先行研究を紹介しつつ自分の研究トピックへと絞り込むステップを確認します。introductionの各情報に合わせて、以下のフローチャートの空所に当てはまる語句を選択肢から選びましょう。すべての選択肢が、いずれかの空所に当てはまります。

1. background: _____ → **2.** previous study: _____ → **3.** present study: _____

> **a.** Designing robot tortoise
> **b.** Introducing gopher tortoises as keystone species
> **c.** Biological threats posed by the decrease of gopher tortoises
> **d.** Various reasons for the decrease in gopher tortoises

✎ Do It Yourself

論文の執筆に際しては、先行研究を調べる必要があります。図書館の蔵書検索をする場合、OPAC (Online Public Access Catalog) を使います。OPACは、館内の端末や自分のパソコンを使って図書館の資料にオンライン・アクセスできる、図書館蔵書目録です。

1. 英語で書かれた研究論文を検索する際に使う、下線を引いた検索用語に当てはまる語句を選択肢から選びましょう。

a. 論文・書籍の著者：_____   d. 論文・書籍の発行年：_____
b. 書籍の版：_____   e. 論文集など雑誌の号：_____
c. 論文・書籍の発行元：_____   f. 国際標準図書番号： ISBN / ISSN

> edition   publisher   issue number
> year of publication   author

2. *The Structure of Scientific Revolutions* という本の初版について、設問1のa、c、dの項目をOPACで調べましょう。

a. _____   c. _____   d. _____

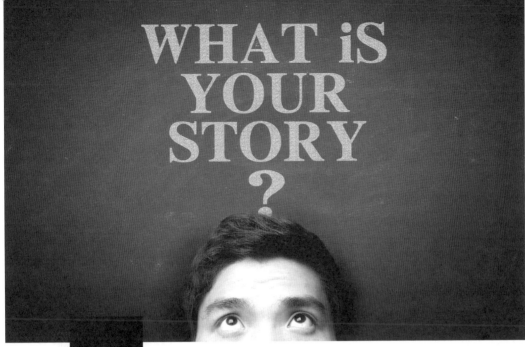

Unit 9

Key Concepts of an Abstract

▶ アブストラクトの重要な特徴

Warm-up Reading

The abstract is a brief summary used by readers to help them judge whether they should read the whole article or not. Because so many articles are published electronically each day, your abstract should be interesting enough to attract readers to read the whole article. An abstract of a research paper should include the study's brief background, purpose, results and methods. It often has a conclusion that may yield further implications. Abstracts normally have strict word limits, which make them challenging to write for inexperienced writers as well as for experienced writers.

☑ Comprehension Check

Warm-up Readingの英文を読み、質問に答えましょう。

1. abstractの役割に当たるものをすべて選びましょう。

☐ To get the reader's attention ☐ To provide a long summary
☐ To receive feedback ☐ To provide a brief summary
☐ To encourage the reader to read further

2. abstractの構成部分でないものを1つ選びましょう。

☐ Purpose ☐ Results
☐ Method ☐ Background
☐ Table of contents ☐ Conclusion

Put It into Practice

▶ Organization

> 論文冒頭（introductionの前）には論文の概略をまとめたabstract（概要・抄録）が付けられます。abstractにも論理的な流れが求められます。厳しい語数制限があるので情報が極限に省かれることもありますが、絶対に欠かせない部分がpurpose（当論文の目的）です。
>
> なお、論文のスタイルは、投稿先学会のルールにより制限を受けます。論文執筆の前にしっかり読み込んでおくことが重要です。abstractの語数制限も、そのうちの1つです。

1. Unit 8でintroductionについて学んだことを参考にし、一般的なabstractの構成部分を論理的な流れになるよう、並べ替えましょう。

[   ] → [   ] → [   ] → [   ]

a. purpose **b.** method and results **c.** background **d.** conclusion

2. 以下は、ある学会の投稿規定からの抜粋です。英文を読んで、後に続く問題a〜dに答えましょう。

When using the IEEE style format, the first (title) page will contain the paper title and each author's name, affiliation, and full address (mailing address, email address, and fax number), with the corresponding author clearly indicated, the abstract (no more than 200 words for regular or survey papers, and 50 words for short papers or communications items), the keywords (index terms), and the beginning of the main text of the paper. A list of significant keywords (also named index terms) should be included in the first page of each submitted paper. Select a minimum of two up to a maximum of five (recommended) keywords ...

http://www.ieee-ras.org/publications/t-ro/information-for-authors

a. タイトルページに含まれるべき情報は何ですか。述べられているものをすべて挙げましょう。

_____

b. corresponding authorとは何ですか。

_____

c. abstractの制限語数については、どのように指示されていますか。

d. keywordについては、どのように指示されていますか。

▶▶ Language

abstractを書く際には、主に現在形、過去形、現在完了形の3つの時制の使い分けが必要です。
・現在形：科学的説明や恒常的真理について述べる
・過去形：個々の検証結果を述べる
・現在完了形：研究背景の説明をする

次ページの英文は、Unit 8 で取り上げた「絶滅危惧種とされるカメ gopher tortoise（アナホリガメ）に代わるロボットカメ開発」に関する論文の abstract から抜粋したものです。下線部の動詞を正しい形に直し、1〜4の英文が何の情報について述べられたものか、選択肢から選んで答えましょう。

a. purpose **b.** background **c.** possible solution **d.** results

1: [   ]
Alongside conservation efforts, one possible solution to the threat posed by the disappearance of the gopher tortoise be →_____ to develop a biomimetic robot capable of producing similar burrows to the gopher tortoise.

2: [   ]
RoboGoph is a digging robot inspired by the gopher tortoise whose populations fall →_____ and they are now classified as "vulnerable."

3: [   ]
We show that the RoboGoph successfully replicate →_____ the tortoise digging motion with an accuracy of over 93.5%.

4: [   ]
We develop →_____ and construct a prototype robot based on observed data of digging motions from actual gopher tortoises.

▶▶▶ Content

> purposeを書く際には、「伝えたい最重要結果・情報」をすべて含めます。限られた時間しかない読者はこの文章だけで内容を理解・判断しようとすることさえあるため、入念に書く必要があります。一言で言うと、その一文に研究全体の「概要」が入っていなければならないのです。

1. 以下のpurposeの英文を読み、どのような研究目的が述べられているか、簡単に日本語で説明しましょう。

    a. Our aim here is to facilitate the automatic detection of cyber attacks on a robotic vehicle.

    _____
    _____

    b. This research is conducted to study the attention characteristics of exhibition visitors, focusing on the presentation method.

    _____
    _____

2. 実際にpurposeの英文を書く練習をしましょう。『ごんぎつね』という昔話があります。文学的解釈抜きで『ごんぎつね』のストーリーの事実のみを説明しましょう。日本語のpurposeに合わせて、与えられた語句を正しい順序に並べかえ、purposeの1文を書いてみましょう。
    この文章だけで必要不可欠な情報は入っているため、読者が『ごんぎつね』を読みたいか読みたくないかの判断が可能という点で、research paperのpurposeと同じです。

    「狐が農夫にしたいたずらを償おうとし、農夫の誤解のために殺される悲劇をここに報告する」

    [the tragedy / apologizing to a farmer for his mischief, / is killed / that a fox, / because of the farmer's misunderstanding / Here we report]

    _____
    _____

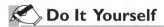 Do It Yourself

purposeの英文を書いてみましょう。

1. 日本語に合わせて空所に適当な表現を書き入れ、英文を完成させましょう。

「実際のアナホリガメの掘削動作の観察データに基づく、ロボットのプロトタイプをここに報告する」

　Here we _____ a prototype robot _____ on observed data of digging _____ from _____ gopher tortoises.

2. 日本語に合わせて、英文を書きましょう。ヒントの表現も参考にしましょう。

「この研究の目的は、頭上のカメラで撮影した画像データを使ってロボットアームをコントロールすることである」

　ヒント：captured by / to control a robotic arm / the image data / overhead

_____
_____
_____

Unit 10

First Draft of Your Abstract

▶ アブストラクトの草稿

Warm-up Reading

　Abstracts normally have strict word limits. Therefore, it is especially challenging to unite sentences using linking words and phrases to create cohesion within such word limits. After you have finished writing a research paper, there are several ways to write the first draft of abstract. Instead of writing from scratch, you may want to collect several sentences from each part of the paper. First, choose several important sentences from each section of a paper. Then put them in logical order. Because you collected those sentences from different sections, they are not properly connected. Once properly connected, they become more cohesive.

☑ Comprehension Check

Warm-up Readingの英文を読み、質問に答えましょう。

1. abstractの書き方を適当な順序に並べ替えましょう。　［　　］→［　　］→［　　］

   a. 適切に文章を繋ぎ、まとまりを出す。
   b. 抜き書きした断片を論理的順序に並べる。
   c. 論文の各セクションから重要な文章を数個抜き書きする。

2. 論文の著者は、常にcohesionを意識しながら論文を書いていかなければなりません。辞書を引かずに、cohesionの意味を英文の文脈から類推して選びましょう。

   a. 文のまとまり
   b. 専門用語
   c. 繋ぎ言葉
   d. 論文のテーマ

Put It into Practice

▶ Organization

abstractは、論文本体を書く前に書くこともできますが、論文本体ができあがっている時は、本体の文を利用して作成することになります。例えば、introductionのbackgroundおよびprevious studiesの部分をまとめてcohesionを作ることで、abstractのbackgroundにすることができます。

Unit 8で取り上げた「絶滅危惧種とされるカメ gopher tortoise（アナホリガメ）に代わるロボットカメ開発」に関する論文のintroductionを読み、backgroundおよびprevious studies（自分たち以外の）について説明している英文はどこからどこまでか、❶〜❽の番号で答えましょう。

___〜___まで

Introduction

第1段落 ❶ The gopher tortoise (*Gopherus kobayashi*) (as shown in Fig. 1) is native to the southeastern region of Crotania and is considered to be a keystone species because the burrows it creates across its habitat provide shelter from high temperatures, forest fires and predators to over 360 different species of animal [1][2].

Fig. 1 gopher tortoise

第2段落 ❷ However, numbers of gopher tortoises have fallen dramatically due to loss of habitat [3], disease [4] and being killed or taken as pets by humans [5]. ❸ At present, they are considered to be a vulnerable species [6]. ❹ This decline in population and the resultant loss of gopher tortoise burrows could thus have a serious negative impact on the ecology of the tortoise's typical habitat.

第3段落 ❺ In previous work [7] we have proposed the biomimetic development of digging robots based on the gopher tortoise that can be used to maintain the necessary number of burrows across the habitat until conservation efforts to restore tortoise populations take effect. ❻ We have successfully analyzed actual tortoise digging motions, identified the component movements and created a control program that can accurately mimic these movements in a simulated test [8].

第4段落 ❼ In this paper we introduce the RoboGoph prototype and validate it by comparing its digging motion with data from actual gopher tortoise digging motions, showing a high level of replication accuracy. ❽ While further development and testing will be necessary before RoboGoph can be considered fit for practical use, the results suggest that RoboGoph could provide a real temporary solution to the current population problem.

▶▶ Language

> 一般に、語数制限の厳しいabstractの草稿作成をする際は、いかにして「短く、かつ効果的に内容を伝えるか」が焦点となります。abstractは、簡潔であると同時に、cohesionが形成されていなければなりません。
>
> cohesionの形成
> ・2つの文を繋げて簡潔な1つの文に：2文の繋がりが「順接」か「逆接」か考える。
> ・既出あるいは衆知の情報を簡潔に：代名詞や定冠詞(the)を用いる。

Organizationのセクションで読んだintroductionを使って、簡潔かつcohesionが形成された英文を作る練習をします。

1. 以下は、❷と❸の2つの一部を繋げて、簡潔な1文にしたものです。aとbに当てはまる語句を選び、文章を完成させましょう。

   However, numbers of gopher tortoises have fallen dramatically, a.(but / and) at present b.(they are / it is) considered to be a vulnerable species.

2. 以下は、❶～❸の3つの文を簡潔にまとめたものです。空所に代名詞を書き入れて、文章を完成させましょう。

   Gopher tortoises and the burrows a._____ dig are considered to be vital to the ecology of b._____ native habitat in the southeastern region of Crotania. However, in recent years ᶜ·_____ populations have fallen and ᵈ·_____ are now classified as "vulnerable."

3. 以下の英文の（　）内の a / an / the から正しいものを選び、文章を完成させましょう。

   a. RoboGoph is (a / an / the) digging robot inspired by the gopher tortoises.

   b. (A / An / The) burrows the gopher tortoises dig are considered to be vital to (a / an / the) ecology of their native habitat in (a / an / the) southeastern region of Crotania.

   c. The purpose of our research is to develop (a / an / the) biomimetic robot capable of producing similar burrows to the gopher tortoises.

▶▶▶ Content

> 全体の流れとその繋がり具合を、読者にはっきりと示す signal expressions が linking words and phrases です。これらは、繋がりの輪郭をはっきりさせる役割を果たします。

以下は、abstract の途中部分です。空所内に当てはまる linking word を選択肢から選び、文章を完成させましょう。文頭に来る語も小文字で示しています。

| alongside | however | now | similar |

Gopher tortoises are considered very important for the ecology of the southeastern region of Crotania. ¹·_____, in recent years their populations have fallen and they are ²·_____ classified as "vulnerable." ³·_____ conservation efforts, one possible solution to the threat posed by the disappearance of the gopher tortoise is to develop a RoboGoph, a biomimetic robot capable of producing ⁴·_____ burrows to the gopher tortoise.

✎ Do It Yourself

以下は「昆虫の減少について」の論文のabstractの冒頭部分です。本章で学習した流れとまとまり、特にcohesionに注意を払いながら、英文を完成させましょう。

　　For more than three decades now, numerous researchers have noted serious declines in the populations of many of the nearly 8000 species of insects. ᵃ_____ reduction has caused concern, because ᵇ_____ are generally regarded as sensitive indicators of our planet's overall health. ᶜ_____, ᵈ_____
_____.

1. 空所a～cに当てはまるlinking wordや代名詞を書き入れましょう。

2. 空所dは、以下の日本語に合わせて英文を作りましょう。

　「今のところ（still）、その理由ははっきりわかっていない」

Unit 11

Rewriting Your Abstract

▶ アブストラクトの最終原稿を仕上げる

📖 Warm-up Reading

One of the most important goals of the abstract is to attract its readers to read the whole paper. For that, you should check and rewrite your own abstract as objectively as possible. Imagining some stranger wrote it, you would then be able to step back and look at your own abstract effectively. Does it make you feel like reading further into the paper? Some writers wait for several days so that they can be more objective than they would be immediately afterwards. This way you can edit your own abstract more drastically.

☑ Comprehension Check

Warm-up Readingの英文を読み、質問に答えましょう。

1. abstractのrewritingの際に重要と述べられているものを、すべて選びましょう。

☐ Be objective
☐ Develop self-checking skills
☐ Edit drastically
☐ Be subjective

2. 自分の writing に客観的になるコツ a と b について、正しい方を選びましょう。

   a. Look at your writing (as objectively as you can / as your own).

   b. Edit (on the day you wrote it / after a while).

Put It into Practice

▶ Organization

Unit 9-10で abstract に入れるべき構成要素について学んできました。最終稿のチェック作業の際は、それらの構成要素の情報が過不足なく含まれていて、かつ論理的な流れに並べられているか確認することが重要です。

以下は、Unit 9以降で取り上げてきた論文 abstract の草稿です。

Abstract

RoboGoph: Utilising Biomimicry in the Development of a Digging Robot Based on a Gopher Tortoise

❶ RoboGoph is a digging robot inspired by the gopher tortoise. ❷ Gopher tortoises and the burrows they dig are considered to be vital to the ecology of their native habitat in the southeastern region of Crotania. ❸ However, in recent years their populations have fallen and they are now classified as "vulnerable." ❹ We develop and construct a prototype robot based on observed data of digging motions from actual gopher tortoises.

1. abstract の重要情報が含まれているか、以下のチェックリストを使って確認しましょう。

> **Check List**
>
> ☐ Is the background stated?
> ☐ Is the purpose stated?
> ☐ Is the background and purpose properly connected?
> ☐ Is the method (experimental approach) stated?
> ☐ Are the results indicated?

2. abstract全体の論の流れがスムーズになるよう、以下の英文を適切な箇所へ挿入します。チェックリストを参考にして、a ～ c を ❶ ～ ❹ の文のどの位置に加えると、文章が論理的に繋がるか答えましょう。

   a. We show that the RoboGoph successfully replicated the tortoise digging motion with an accuracy of over 93.5%. [　　　　　]

   b. The performance of the prototype was analyzed and compared to the original gopher tortoise data. [　　　　　]

   c. Alongside conservation efforts, one possible solution to the threat posed by the disappearance of the gopher tortoise is to develop a RoboGoph, a biomimetic robot capable of producing similar burrows to the gopher tortoise. [　　　　　]

▶▶ Language

最終チェックで大切なことの1つに、英語での数字の表現があります。以下のルールに則って、数字はスペルアウトするかアラビア数字を使います。
- 文頭の数字は必ずスペルアウトする。
- 文頭の大きな数字は、できれば文中に入れ込むよう文全体を書き換え、アラビア数字を使うと良い。
- 10未満のアラビア数字はスペルアウトする。（10をスペルアウトする場合もある。）
- アラビア数字とスペルアウトされた数字がひとつの文中に混在する場合、アラビア数字に統一する。

以下の英文について、数字や文章で修正した方が良いところがあれば修正し、なければC (Correct) と答えましょう。文章全体を書き換える問題もあります。

1. We have to write a report of about 7 pages in length.

2. Six hundred and seventeen patients were examined in the experiment.

3. There were one hundred and twenty-five people in the room.

4. The vote was 185 in favor of the action and only nine opposed.

5. The TBB television station is Channel Thirteen.

6. Every morning at nine o'clock the bells rang.

▶▶▶ Content

情報を流れよく、かつ間違いなく伝える必要があるabstractでは、語数削減に熱心なあまり、書き直しの途中で、しばしば削除できないものまで消してしまうことが起こります。その結果、文章のparallelism（パラレリズム）形式を崩し、内容に誤解を生じさせることがあります。文章のparallelismとは、並列した言葉が全体に一定のパターンを与え、類似の形式を与えることを指します。

- ○ Ken likes swimming, jogging and playing tennis.
- × Ken likes to swim, jogging and tennis.

- ○ The area of Alaska is greater than that of California.
- × The area of Alaska is greater than California.

最終チェックの際には、文章のparallelismに問題がないかもチェックしましょう。

また、接続詞andなどで複数の語句を並列させて繋ぐ長い英文を作る場合は、できるだけ短い語句から長い語句へと並べ、文の流れを妨げないようにします。

1. 以下の英文はparallelismが崩れています。必要な語句を補って文を整えましょう。

   a. The mean gain scores for students in the experimental group were greater than students in the control group.

   b. Our conclusions are consistent with Brown et al.

2. 長い英文のparallelismをチェックします。英文aとbのうち、文の流れがよりスムーズなのはどちらでしょうか。

   a. The loss of gopher tortoise burrows will affect organisms, such as rabbits and insects, that depend on shelter provided by the burrows, and forests.

   b. The loss of gopher tortoise burrows will affect forests and organisms, such as rabbits and insects, that depend on shelter provided by the burrows.

Do It Yourself

以下は、間違いを含む文章です。主語と動詞の呼応、代名詞、数字、parallelism などについて検討し、下線の部分が間違っていれば訂正しましょう。

1. After an average of 4 front-to-back digging motion, the tortoise switches and digging with the opposite front leg.

2. The burrows those creates across its habitat provides shelter from high temperatures, forest fires and predators to over 360 different species of animal.

3. One possible solution to the threat posed by the disappearance of the gopher tortoise are to develop a RoboGoph, a biomimetic robot capable of producing similar to the gopher tortoise.

Unit 12

Key Concepts of Presentations

▶ プレゼンテーションの基本的特徴

📖 Warm-up Reading

During your academic career, you may be required to present your research in the classroom or at conferences. Presenting your work is important for sharing your ideas with a wider audience. It can also attract attention to your work or paper. Unlike written communication, your audience has only one chance to hear your speech in oral communication. Therefore, in addition to the content, you will have to talk clearly, sometimes with effective gestures, and tell your ideas in a simple way so that your audience can follow your presentation.

☑ Comprehension Check

Warm-up Readingの英文を読み、質問に答えましょう。

1. 自分の研究を発表できるようになることはなぜ重要だと述べられていますか。日本語で答えましょう。

2. presentationと論文での発表の違いは何だと述べられていますか。日本語で答えましょう。

_____

_____

3. 効果的なpresentationをする際に必要なことをすべて選びましょう。
☐ Speak in a quiet voice
☐ Use complicated expressions that can overwhelm your audience
☐ Tell your ideas clearly so that your audience can keep up
☐ Use gestures when needed

Put It into Practice

▶ Organization

presentationをする際は、目の前の聴衆を意識しなければならないため、原稿の構成や言葉遣いにおいてessayやresearch paperと異なる部分があります。

以下は、presentationをする際の重要なポイントを述べたものです。空所にあてはまる語句を選んで、書き入れましょう。

| simple | well-organized | needs |

- **Focus on what your audience** [1.] _____ .
  As you prepare the presentation, you need to always keep in mind what the audience wants to know.
- **Keep your message** [2.] _____ .
  You should always keep your key message focused and brief.
- **Make your transcript** [3.] _____ .
  Organize your presentation like a story. Stories help your audience pay attention and follow your ideas.

▶▶ Language

> presentation は聴衆を前にして行なわれるため、その内容に入る前や内容を述べ終わった後に、挨拶や自己紹介、聴衆に対する謝辞などを述べるのが一般的です。

以下の英文は、「ハーネス一体型盲導犬用ドッグ・パック(Dog Pack)の開発」に関するpresentationのintroduction（導入部）とclosing（結び）のscript（発表原稿）です。言語や表現の特徴を考察してみましょう。

introduction

❶ I'm Yoshiki Ando. ❷ I will present our work on a "user-friendly, all-in-one harness and dog pack for guide dogs." ❸

closing

That's all for my presentation. ❹ Thank you for your attention.

1. 主語は何人称が使われていますか。

    ＿＿＿＿＿人称

2. 以下の挨拶表現は❶〜❹のどこに加えれば良いでしょうか。
    a. I'd like to express my sincere thanks to the guide dogs and their users. [   ]
    b. Hello everyone. [   ]
    c. I'm very glad to have a chance to talk to you about my research today. [   ]

All-in-one harness and dog pack

▶▶▶ Content

> presentationにおいて、発表する内容に専門的知識が含まれる場合に、専門用語を用いることがよくあります。聴衆にとって初めてと思われる用語は、聴衆の理解度に合わせて、言い換えや例え、比較を用いると良いでしょう。
>
> 　特に比較は、最も分かりやすい情報提示法のひとつです。例えば、新旧を比較することで、両者の「類似性」や「相違性」をより明確に分析して伝えることができます。また、2つの物を比較して述べながら、「利点」と「欠点」などを明らかにすることもできます。

1. 以下はOrganizationのセクションで挙げたpresentationのscriptで、「ハーネス一体型盲導犬用ドッグ・パック」について説明している部分です。空所に入る英文aとbを作成し、scriptを完成させましょう。

　You might not know what a dog pack is. ___**a**___ . Also, ___**b**___ . The certificate which shows "this dog is on duty" is inserted here in this bag.

a. It's _____ for _____ ,
such as plastic poop bags, a pack of tissues, and a coagulant for feces
「それは排泄物収納用プラスチックバッグやティッシュペーパー、排泄物凝固剤といった、イヌ関連用品を運ぶのに使われます」
Notes: poop bag「排泄物収納用バッグ」　coagulant「凝固剤」　feces「排泄物」

b. It's _____ for keeping _____
_____
「それはイヌとユーザーが清潔かつ安全でいられるようにするには、なくてはならないものです」

2. 以下は設問1で取り上げた「ハーネス一体型盲導犬用ドッグ・パック」と比較させるために、「従来型の盲導犬用ドッグ・パック」について説明している部分です。空所に入る語句を選択肢から選んで書き入れ、scriptを完成させましょう。

the bracing handle	gestural signals
the increased weight	detachable-type

　Let's take a look at this picture. A conventional ᵃ·_____ of dog pack is attached to ᵇ _____ of the dog harness. The dog seems uncomfortable because ᶜ· _____ of the bracing handle with the dog pack makes it difficult for the dog to pick up ᵈ· _____ sent by the user.

Unit 12 Key Concepts of Presentations　59

Do It Yourself

1. 以下は、Contentのセクションで作成した2つのscriptです。これらのscriptを使って、presentationの練習をしてみましょう。presentationでは、聴衆に伝わっているかどうかを確認しながら話す必要があります。適切に間を空け、聴衆が理解できるようスピードにも配慮しながら話しましょう。

間を空ける箇所については、以下のルールを参照し、scriptの間を空けるところにスラッシュ（/）を入れて、声に出して読んでみましょう。

> ① ピリオドやカンマの後
> ② 接続詞の前
> ③ 長い主語の後
> ④ 長い関係詞節や名詞句の前

You might not know what a dog pack is. It's used for carrying dog-related items, such as plastic poop bags, a pack of tissues, and a coagulant for feces and it's essential for keeping the dogs and their users clean and safe.

Let's take a look at this picture. A conventional detachable-type of dog pack is attached to the bracing handle of the dog harness. The dog seems uncomfortable because the increased weight of the bracing handle with the dog pack makes it difficult for the dog to pick up gestural signals sent by the user.

2. 以下は、"Problems Caused by E-Waste" という発表のscriptの一部です。日本語を英語に直して空所に書き入れ、scriptを完成させましょう。また、出来上がったscriptを声に出して読んでみましょう。

a. _____ . It describes b. _____
_____. c. _____
_____ has become a source of income in developing countries. However, the process of recycling it exposes workers to d. _____
_____ which are likely to e. _____
_____ .

    a. e-wasteとは何かご存知ないかも知れません
    b. 廃棄された電子、電気機器
    c. e-wasteに含まれる貴重な要素をリサイクルすること
    d. 鉛（lead）やカドミウム（cadmium）のような多くの危険な物質
    e. 人間の健康に影響を及ぼす

Unit 13

Preparing Visual Aids
▶ 視覚資料の作成

📖 Warm-up Reading

　Giving a good academic presentation is quite different from writing a good academic paper. As you only have one chance to give a presentation before the audience, visual aids help them process the information more easily. Graphs, tables, diagrams, bullet points and so on, are all visual aids. The best visual aids do not distract from the speaker, but enhance what he or she is saying. Each slide should not contain too much information (it may be better to put this information on a handout) and the flow of this information should be controlled. Remember: visual aids are for the audience, not the presenter.

☑ Comprehension Check

Warm-up Reading の英文を読み、質問に答えましょう。

1. visual aids（視覚資料）を提供する目的は何だと述べられていますか。日本語で答えましょう。

_____

_____

2. the best visual aids の特徴として述べられているものをすべて選びましょう。

☐ Using many words in one slide
☐ Containing relevant information
☐ Supporting the presenter's ideas
☐ Using many graphics for attracting audience attention

Put It into Practice

▶ Organization

> スライドは聴衆の理解を促す重要なツールです。発表時間や内容の密度に応じてスライドは過不足なく準備する必要があります。essay や research paper の構成同様に、スライドの構成要素も重要です。script の構成に沿ってもっとも必要な visual aids を選び、適切な情報量に制限して見やすく提示しましょう。

以下は、2つの発表用スライドと、その情報の過不足や見やすさについて日本語で評価を述べたものです。空所に適当な語句を書き入れましょう。

slide A	slide B
Our proposed prototype is shown in this picture. It's an all-in-one harness and dog pack. Its key features are a simple design made from materials that are soft, light and washable.	**Our proposed prototype** ・An all-in-one harness and dog pack ・Simple design ・Soft, light and washable material

slide A　　　　　　　　　　　　　　**slide B**

slide A は ^{1.}＿＿＿＿＿＿＿＿＿＿が多すぎ、また文章がそのまま載せられており、聴衆には見づらい。一方、slide B は ^{2.}＿＿＿＿＿＿＿＿＿＿で提示されており、情報が整理されていて見やすい。

▶▶ Language

🖉 スライドは、伝える内容のポイントを列挙するような場合はbullet points format（箇条書きフォーマット）が好まれ、内容に応じて名詞句、主語が省略された動詞で始まる句、文など適切な提示方法が選ばれます。また、それぞれの項目はparallelism、つまり同じスタイルで書かれますので、名詞句なら名詞句、命令文なら命令文で統一されます。

1. 以下のスライドの空所に入る語句の組み合わせとして、もっとも適切な表現を選びましょう。

Purpose of the research

- _____ problems of conventional packs by conducting interviews

- _____ a user-friendly poop bag holder based on the analysis of the survey results

   a. Identification / Development
   b. To identify / To develop
   c. Identified / Developed

2. 以下のスライドの下線部a〜cの動詞を、適切な形に直しましょう。

Quantitative data

- Typically collected with surveys or questionnaires
- Often ^{a.} perceive → _____ as a more objective method of data analysis
- ^{b.} Require → _____ to use of statistical analysis
- Counted or ^{c.} express _____ numerically

▶▶▶ Content

> visual aidsは、文字情報だけでなく、伝えたい情報によってグラフ、図、絵、写真、表など様々なものを用います。

1. 以下の visual aids の名称を、選択肢から選んで答えましょう。

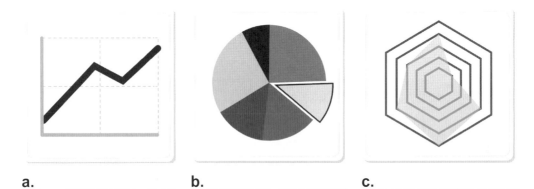

a. _____　b. _____　c. _____

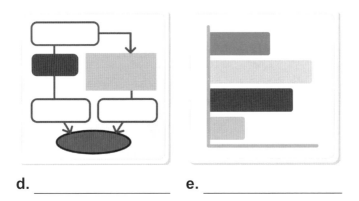

d. _____　e. _____

> bar graph　　radar chart　　line graph　　pie chart　　flow chart

2. 以下の情報を visual aids にする場合、どれを用いて表すのがもっとも適切か、選択肢から選んで答えましょう。

a. Comparison of a conventional dog pack and a new product
_____

b. Growth rate of the number of dog pack users　_____
c. Design of a dog pack for guide dogs　_____
d. Schedule of a guide dog training project　_____

> flow chart　　picture　　graph　　table

Do It Yourself

以下は「盲導犬用ドッグ・パック」の従来製品と新製品について説明をしたscriptとそのスライドです。scriptをもとに、スライドの空所1～9に適切な情報を書き入れ、スライドを完成させましょう。

Conventional dog packs consist of a leather belt and a cloth dog pack, and weigh about 540 grams. Gestural signals sent to a guide dog by the owner are transmitted through the structure. Only the cloth holder can be washed. On the other hand, the prototype model of the new dog pack weighs only approximately 220 grams. Both the harness and dog pack are made of washable mesh fabric. The materials used in the construction mean that the guide dog owner's signals can be transmitted more easily to the dog.

Comparison of the 2 models

	Model A (conventional)	Model B (prototype)
Materials	Belt: 1. [　　　　] Dog pack: cloth	Harness: 2. [　　　　] Dog pack: 3. [　　　　]
Gestural Signals	Transmittable	4. [　　　　] transmittable
Weight	Approx. 5. [　　　　]	Approx. 6. [　　　　]
Cleaning	Only 7. [　　　　]	Both 8. [　　　　] and 9. [　　　　]

Unit 14

Finishing Your Scripts

▶ 発表原稿の完成

📖 Warm-up Reading

When you have decided a topic for your presentation, check how much time you have been given and then write out the presentation roughly first. You should be careful when preparing the structure of your talk. It is necessary to decide on the main points you want to emphasize. You also need to avoid including irrelevant information and try to make the talk flow smoothly. It would be better to use signal expressions so that audiences can easily follow your presentation.

☑ Comprehension Check

Warm-up Reading の英文を読み、質問に答えましょう。

1. presentation の topic（主題）を決めてからすべきことは何だと述べられていますか。日本語で答えましょう。

_____

_____

2. presentationの心得として良いと思われるものは何か、当てはまるものをすべて選びましょう。

☐ Make the talk longer than the allotted time to help the audience understand the content.
☐ Include a lot of information whether it is relevant or irrelevant to the topic.
☐ Organize the information for the audience to easily understand.
☐ Prevent the talk from often going off track.

Put It into Practice

▶ Organization

academic presentationの構成はessayと同様、大きく分けて3つに分かれます。さらに細かく分けると、8つの構成要素から成ります。この構成に従うと、聴衆にとって情報の流れが掴みやすくなり、内容が伝わりやすくなります。

以下の表はpresentationの構成を説明したものです。

Introduction（序論）	① Greetings（挨拶）、Self-introduction（自己紹介）
	② Introduction（導入）
	❸ Research Background（研究の背景・経緯）
	❹ Research Purpose（研究の目的）
Body（本論）	❺ Research Method（研究方法）
	❻ Result（研究結果）
Conclusion（結論）	⑦ Conclusion（結論）
	⑧ Closing（結びの言葉）

以下は、「ハーネス一体型盲導犬用ドッグ・パックの開発」に関するpresentationのscriptの一部です。a〜cが、表の❸〜❻のどの構成要素に当てはまるか答えましょう。

a: [   ]
　Our proposed prototype is shown in this picture on the right. It's an all-in-one harness and dog pack. Its key features are a simple design made from materials that are soft, light and washable.

b: [   ]
　We had the guide dog users trial two models of dog packs: a conventional

model and our proposed design.

C: [   ]

To begin with, I'm going to talk about the background of my research. Previous surveys have shown that some people using conventional dog packs for their guide dogs complain that they are inconvenient. So it's necessary for us to develop a user-friendly dog pack for users and their dogs as well.

▶▶ Language

presentationでは、聴衆の注意を喚起するため、また何について言及しているのかを分かりやすくするための、特徴的なsignal expressionsが使われます。こうした表現をscriptに効果的に入れ込むことによって、スライド提示のタイミングや、進行がスムーズになります。

以下のsignal expressionsを、役割によってグループ分けしましょう。

> Let's take ~ as one example   Let's talk about ~   In conclusion, ~
> To begin with, ~   For instance, take a look at ~
> Let's take a look at this picture.   Let me explain my study on ~

1. 話を切り出す _____

2. 例示する _____

3. スライドの切り替えを示す _____

4. 結論を述べる _____

▶▶▶ Content

> 発表を聴衆に分かりやすくするには、伝えたい内容を整理し、簡潔にまとめて提示する必要があります。要点をまとめるには、情報を列挙したり、新・旧の情報を順番に提示したりなどすると良いでしょう。また、関連のない情報を排除することも必要です。

1. 以下は、「ハーネス一体型盲導犬用ドッグ・パックの開発」に関するpresentationのscriptで、「研究の背景」について述べている部分です。scriptの冒頭に入る語句を選択肢から選びましょう。また、不要な情報を見つけ下線を引きましょう。

   _____ A conventional detachable-type of dog pack is attached to the bracing handle of the dog harness. The guide dogs are trained to be well-behaved. Our proposed prototype is an all-in-one harness and dog pack. The encircling design of the soft core materials of the harness is able to reduce dog pack's weight and the size, which lessens the burden on both the users and their dogs.

   > a. Let me show you how to use the dog pack.
   > b. Let's take a look at these two models.
   > c. Let's go back to the picture of the conventional type of dog pack.

2. 以下のscriptは、「研究の目的」を列挙している部分です。presentationでvisual aidsを用いて聴衆に提示する際にどのようなフレーズを用いれば良いか、下線部に入る適切なものを選択肢から選びましょう。

   _____; To identify problems of conventional packs by conducting interviews and to develop a user-friendly dog pack based on the analysis of the survey results.

   > a. These research targets are
   > b. Our research focuses on these problems
   > c. Our research targets are as follows

Do It Yourself

以下の発表原稿案の template（定型書式）に基づいて、presentation の script を作ります。1～4の空所には当てはまるものを選択肢から選び、下線部 a～d には適当な語句を考えて書き入れましょう。Organization のセクションで学んだ、presentation の構成を意識して答えましょう。

> **Topic:** Health and Exercise
> **Title:** Short Exercises Help You Stay Healthy
> **The points you want to emphasize:** Medical expenses are increasing every year. We have to individually tackle this problem. An article from BBC News says that 15 minutes of daily exercise is the bare minimum for our health.

Hello everyone. I'm Koki Tanaka. I'm going to talk to you about a. _____.

[1. ____] In Japan, b. _____ and the number of young people who suffer from diseases is also increasing. So I feel that c. _____. We know exercise is good for health, but we don't know how much or how intense it should be. I wanted to know what's the most efficient way for us to exercise.

[2. ____] I searched the internet and found an article from BBC News that d. _____. According to the article, a couch potato lifestyle, like watching TV for six hours a day, can shorten your lifespan by five years, while 15 minutes per day of moderate exercise, such as brisk walking, can add three years to your life expectancy. That's all that we need to do every day and it's easy to do.

[3. ____]

[4. ____] That's all for my presentation. Thank you for your attention.

> **A.** Next, let me show you how I investigated this question.
> **B.** In conclusion, I recommend that we all exercise for just 15 minutes each day, for ourselves and our country.
> **C.** To begin with, I'd like to talk about why I chose this topic.
> **D.** The result is that if we all can stay healthy for as long as possible, our quality of life will be boosted and medical expenses will also be reduced.

Unit 15

Evaluating Your Presentation

▶ プレゼンテーションの評価

📖 Warm-up Reading

How do you know whether your presentation is good or bad? Because it is difficult to see yourself present, it can be difficult to evaluate yourself. The first step is to watch other people presenting and to evaluate for yourself whether they did well or poorly. After that, practice is important. If you can ask a friend or colleague to watch one of your practices and give you feedback, this can help you to improve. Lastly, recording your practice, watching the video and evaluating your own performance can also be very effective. Sufficient preparation leads to a successful presentation.

☑ Comprehension Check

Warm-up Readingの英文を読み、質問に答えましょう。

1. presentationの出来の良し悪しを判断できるようになるためには、どうすべきだと述べられていますか。日本語で答えましょう。

2. presentationの技術を改善するためには、どうすべきだと述べられていますか。日本語で答えましょう。

_____

_____

📝 Put It into Practice

▶ Organization

🖉 presentationを評価する際は、Rubric（ルーブリック）という評価基準が用いられることがあります。

評価基準　Poor = 1
　　　　　Adequate = 2
　　　　　Good = 3
　　　　　Excellent = 4

以下は、Presentation Rubric（プレゼンテーションの評価基準）からの抜粋です。a～cのどれがOrganizationの評価基準か選び、どういった点が評価されるのかを答えましょう。

a.
Poor: Explanation is often difficult to understand. Many spelling and punctuation errors.
Excellent: Explanation is almost always easy to understand. Almost no spelling or punctuation errors.

b.
Poor: Little or no eye contact; unclear, monotone voice; negative body language.
Excellent: Very consistent eye contact; clear voice with natural intonation and stress; positive body language.

c.
Poor: No clear structure (introduction, body, conclusion); ideas are ordered illogically.
Excellent: Very clear structure (introduction, body, conclusion); ideas are always logically ordered.

　　Organizationの評価基準：_____

▶▶ Language

presentationの最後には、たいてい発表内容に対するQuestions & Answers（質疑応答）の時間が設けられます。Questions & Answersの内容もpresentationの評価に入ると考えた方が良いでしょう。ここでは、「質問に的確に答えているかどうか」が評価されます。どのような質問が出てくるのか前もって準備をしておき、答えが分からない場合でも率直に対応しましょう。

以下はQuestions & Answersでよく使われる表現です。日本語を英語に直しましょう。

1. Sorry, I couldn't catch what you said. _____?
   「もう一度質問を繰り返していただけますか」

2. _____
   "whether education through the internet is possible or not." Is that right?
   「あなたのご質問は〜です」

3. Thank you very much _____
   _____.
   「重要な質問をしていただいたことを」

4. _____
    more about our research project.
   「説明させてください」

5. Sorry, I don't have much time to answer your question. _____
   _____?
   「後ほどお話しさせていただいてもよろしいでしょうか」

6. _____, but we're going to continue our investigation.
   「今はそのご質問の答えを持ち合わせておりません」

▶▶▶ Content

> 発表内容の評価は、visual aids が口頭での説明を適切に補っているかどうかによっても左右されます。内容に合わない資料はただ聴衆の気をそらせるだけであるため、必要と思われるものを抽出して提示します。

以下は、「ハーネス一体型盲導犬用ドッグ・パックの開発」に関する presentation の script の一部です。1と2が、a〜d のどのスライドに当てはまるか答えましょう。

1. Our proposed prototype is shown in this picture. It's an all-in-one harness and dog pack. Its key features are a simple design made from materials that are soft, light and washable. [   ]

2. We had the guide dog users trial two models of dog packs: a conventional model and our proposed design and observed the informants using harnesses with their dogs in April and October in 2015 and in January in 2016. [   ]

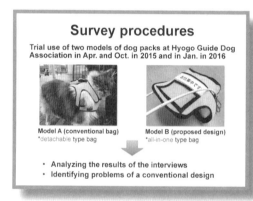

a.

b.

c.

d.

Do It Yourself

あなたが行ったpresentationに対して、巻末のPresentation Rubricを用いて、以下のような評価を受けました。

Organization	5
Language	4
Visual aids	2
Presentation skills	2

あなたの発表は、Organizationは問題が無く、Languageはまだ少しチェックが不十分だった可能性があります。改善が必要なのは、Visual aidsとPresentation skillsです。以下のPresentation Rubricの該当箇所を参考にして、それぞれどのような問題があったのか考えましょう。

	Adequate = 2
Visual Aids	Design of visual aids sometimes makes presentation hard to follow.
Presentation Skills	Inconsistent eye contact; somewhat unclear, monotone voice; neutral body language.

Visual aidsの問題点

_____

_____

Presentation skillsの問題点

_____

_____

Unit 15 Evaluating Your Presentation

巻末資料

Signal Expressions for Academic Writing

academic writing に頻出の signal expressions（合図表現）のリストです。各章で取り上げられている表現以外のものも含めた重要な signal expressions を、introduction や body などの構成要素ごとにまとめています。writing 活動に必要な表現を探したり、Organization を意識した表現の確認をしたりなど、授業の内外で活用しましょう。

Check List

academic writing において、自分で書いた学術的な文章を推敲したり、文章に目を通し校正したりする活動は大変重要です。この Check List を用いて自分の文章をチェックすることで、客観的に見直し、また、おさえておくべきポイントは何かを確認することができます。peer review の際にもこれらの Check List を活用しましょう。

Presentation Rubric

rubric とは、ある課題についての学習到達状況を評価するための「基準」を示したものです。presentation を行う際にこの Presentation Rubric を用いることによって、発表内容や視覚資料などのどういった点が評価されるのか、その評価基準を、発表者と聴衆の双方が共有することができます。

Signal Expressions for Academic Writing

以下は、academic writing に頻出の signal expressions（合図表現）のリストです。signal expressions は、後に続く情報をあらかじめ合図する役割を持っている表現で、後続情報を効果的に導入したり、前出の情報と後続情報を繋いだりする役割を果たします。

Essay
Abstract にも利用することができるものが含まれています。

■Title

何かのプロセスを示す	How to ...
	Process / Procedure of ...
何かを分類する	Types / Styles / Kinds / Classification of ...
因果関係を分析する	Effects of ... / A major cause of / The origin of ...
	Cause and effect between ...
	An investigation into the cause of ...
	Establishing the cause of ...
	Identification of the cause of ...
何かを比較対照して分析する	A comparative study of ...
	The comparison between X and Y
	A striking contrast in ...
	A contrastive study of ...
問題解決の提案をする	Solving ...
	A solution strategy of ...

■Introduction

background	一般的な情報を示す	There are several major steps involved in ...
		Impressing your friends is easy when you follow ...
		The idea that ... is becoming increasingly common.
		It is important to consider both the advantages and disadvantages of ...
	データや事実などを提示する	According to a number of studies / surveys, ...
		Some experts / researchers claim that ...
		pointed out in the article / essay / paper titled "..." that ...
	引用や逸話を入れる	It is often said that "If you run after two hares, you will catch neither."
		Baron, a two-year old dog, won official commendation for ...
	読者の知らない情報を定義する	... is / are / refer(s) to ... that / to V / V-ing / V-ed

background	読者の注意を喚起する	Why do these problems persists?
		What is causing this problem?
thesis statement	筆者の主張を述べる	I will explore ...
		I will focus on ...
		This essay argues that ...
outline	主要な論点を箇条書きにして示す	I will put forward three possible benefits before discussing ...
	どのように論を進めるかを示す	This essay attempts to ...
		This paper examines / discusses ...

■ Body

順序やプロセスを書く	first / second / finally, every time, whenever, soon after that
	as soon as, meanwhile, from then on, after that, at this point
	the first step / the next step / the last step
分類する	There are three kinds / types / classes of ...
	We can divide / classify / categorize / group ... into two kinds / types.
	... can be divided / classified / categorized / grouped into ...
因果関係を示す	As a result of, Consequently, due to, because of, as a consequence of ...
	because, since, for this reason, so, therefore, thus
比較を表す	Both A and B are, Likewise, Similarly, alike
	as ... as, the same as, similar to, like
対照を表す	Although, Even though, However, Whereas

■ Conclusion

brief background	... usually results in ...
	... is often said to be the main cause of ...
	As I stated earlier,
sum-up	I have found that ...
	In conclusion,
	To conclude, To sum up,
	All in all, Therefore, All things considered, On the whole,
solution, suggestion or prediction	One solution to solve the problem is to ...
	The evidence suggests that ...
	... might be a possible future alternative to ...

Abstract

Essayのsignal expressionsの中にもAbstractに利用することができるものが含まれています。

■Background

一般的な背景を紹介する	It is widely accepted that ...
背景として最近の研究を紹介する	Recent studies show that ...
当該分野の傾向を紹介する	... is considered to be ...
	Much research in recent years has focused on ...
	Numerous experiments have established that ...
先行研究を紹介する	... discovered that ...
	... indicated that ...

■Purpose

本研究の目的を述べる	Here we report that ...
	In this paper, we describe that ...
	This paper focuses on ...
	The purpose of this study is to describe and examine ...
	This paper introduces ...
	In the present study, we performed ...
新しく開発した事柄を報告する	We develop ...
	New ... was developed ...

■Method

研究方法を紹介する	... was / were determined / suggested / verified / treated ...
研究方法の詳細を紹介する	... was / were formulated / evaluated / used / measured to decide / identify ...

■Results

結果を示す	... was achieved / observed / obtained / found
	It was noted that ...

Presentation Slide

■Visual Aids

visual aidsについて説明する	As you can see in this picture, ...
	This graph shows ...
	If we look at these numbers, we see ...

スライドに聴衆の注意を向ける	Please look at this slide.
	Just take a look at this picture.
	Let's take a look at this graph.
	Let's see how this looks.
スライド上に複数ある特定のvisual aidsに聴衆の注意を向ける	Let's look at this bar graph on the right / on the left / in the middle / at the bottom.

Presentation Script

■ Introduction

プレゼンテーションを開始する	I will present ...
	I'm going to talk about ...
プレゼンテーションの概要を述べる	Let me start by telling you briefly about my research.
	Here is the outline of my presentation.
聴衆に専門用語を導入する	You might not know what ... is.
	Has anyone heard about ... ?
	Let me explain what ... is.
研究の背景を述べる	Previous surveys have shown that ...
	I'm going to give you some background infomation about ...

■ Body

研究の方法を述べる	In order to identify existing problems, we carried out interviews with the users and observed them using ...
研究の結果を述べる	Our proposed prototype is shown in this picture.
	This is our solution to the problem.
	We found out that ...
話題を切り替え、次の要点に移る	Let's move on to the next topic.
	Let's go back to this data.

■ Conclusion

要約を述べる	Let me summarize the points.
プレゼンテーションを終了する	Thank you very much.
	Thank you very much for your attention.

Check List for Essay

▼ Organization

Introduction
- [ ] Some general background to the title（導入としての一般知識・背景）
- [ ] Thesis statement（この文章で述べたいこと）
- [ ] Outline（この文章の概略）

Body
- [ ] Clear topic sentence（明確な主張：トピックセンテンス）
- [ ] Ideas supported with details and examples（例を挙げた詳しい支持文）

Conclusion
- [ ] Brief background of the theme（エッセイの簡単な背景）
- [ ] Summed-up main ideas of the paragraphs（この文章の主なまとめ）
- [ ] Concluding suggestion/prediction/solution（結論や予測的見解、問題の解決策）

▼ Language
- [ ] Word choice（語彙選択が適切である）
- [ ] Punctuation（句読点が正しく用いられている）
- [ ] Pronoun Reference（代名詞が指しているものが明確である）
- [ ] Spelling（スペルミスがない）
- [ ] Capitalization（大文字の使い方が適切である）
- [ ] Missing Word（単語が抜け落ちていない）
- [ ] Sentence Structure（構文が正しく使えている）
- [ ] Verb Tense（時制が合っている）
- [ ] Fused (run-on) Sentence（接続詞無しに文が繋がっていない）
- [ ] Antecedent Agreement（関係代名詞の先行詞との呼応が正しい）
- [ ] Sentence Fragment（文が完全文になっている）
- [ ] Subject-verb Agreement（主語と動詞の呼応）
- [ ] Number Agreement（数が一致している）
- [ ] Use of appropriate transition words to aid flow
（情報がスムーズに流れるように適当な繋ぎ言葉が使われている）

▼ Content
- [ ] Full and rich development of content（内容が濃い）
- [ ] Focusing on the theme（テーマから離れていない、余分な情報が含まれていない）
- [ ] Sufficient explanation and supporting information （テーマの支持情報が充分にある）
- [ ] Clearly stated positions（筆者の視点が明らか）
- [ ] Not using too many citations from sources（引用が多すぎない）
- [ ] No plagiarism（盗用がない）

Check List for Abstract

▼ Organization（標準的な情報の流れ）
- [ ] Accurate, concise and informative title（正確で簡潔、十分な情報を含んだタイトル）
- [ ] Authors' details including information such as affiliation and email address
  （所属、emailアドレスなどの著者情報）
- [ ] Brief background of research（研究の簡単な背景）
- [ ] Clearly stated purpose（明確に述べられた目的）
- [ ] Methods stating how and what you did（どのような方法で何をしたのかを述べる）
- [ ] Summarized main results（主な結果のまとめ）
- [ ] Concluding statement（結論の提示）
- [ ] Relevant keywords that will help researchers find your paper
  （検索の手助けになるキーワード）

▼ Language
- [ ] Word choice（語彙選択が適切である）
- [ ] Punctuation（句読点が正しく用いられている）
- [ ] Pronoun Reference（代名詞が指しているものが明確である）
- [ ] Spelling（スペルミスがない）
- [ ] Capitalization（大文字の使い方が適切である）
- [ ] Missing Word（単語が抜け落ちていない）
- [ ] Sentence Structure（構文が正しく使えている）
- [ ] Verb Tense（時制が合っている）
- [ ] Run-on Sentence（接続詞無しに文が繋がっていない）
- [ ] Antecedent Agreement（関係代名詞の先行詞との呼応が正しい）
- [ ] Sentence Fragment（文が完全文になっている）
- [ ] Subject-verb Agreement（主語と動詞が呼応している）
- [ ] Number Agreement（数が一致している）
- [ ] Use of appropriate transition words to aid flow
  （情報がスムーズに流れるように適当な繋ぎ言葉が使われている）

▼ Content
- [ ] Keeping to submission guidelines including number of words
  （語数を含め投稿規定に沿ったものとなっている）
- [ ] Including key parts of abstract: title and author information, background, purpose, methods, results, conclusions and keywords（重要な構成部分が含まれている：タイトルと著者情報、研究の背景・目的・方法・結果・結論、キーワードリスト）
- [ ] Short and concise（簡潔で正確である）
- [ ] Previously unpublished data（未発表の内容である）
- [ ] No plagiarism（盗用がない）

Check List for Presentation

▼ Organization

Introduction
- [ ] Greetings, self-introduction（挨拶、自己紹介）
- [ ] Introduction to your presentation（発表の導入）
- [ ] Some general background（研究の背景・経緯、このテーマを選んだ理由）
- [ ] Research Purpose（研究の目的）

Body
- [ ] Research method（研究の方法）
- [ ] Research results（研究結果、実験結果、何が分かったか）

Conclusion
- [ ] Summed-up main ideas of your presentation（発表内容の要約）
- [ ] Concluding suggestion / prediction / solution（結論、予測的見解、問題の解決策）
- [ ] Closing（結びの言葉、謝辞）

▼ Language (Script)

- [ ] Greetings, self-introduction（挨拶の言葉や自己紹介の言葉は適切か）
- [ ] No irrelevant information（不要な情報がないか）
- [ ] No complicated expressions（分かりにくい表現はないか）
- [ ] Pronunciation（単語の発音は適切か）
- [ ] Closing（結びの言葉は適切か）

▼ Language (Visual Aids)

- [ ] Not using too many words（文字が多すぎない）
- [ ] Using appropriate size of letters（文字の大きさが適切である）
- [ ] Spelling（スペルミスがない）
- [ ] Capitalization（大文字の使い方が適切である）
- [ ] Missing Word（単語が抜け落ちていない）
- [ ] Punctuation（句読点が正しく用いられている）
- [ ] Using appropriate signal expressions（適切な合図表現を使用している）
- [ ] Containing relevant information（無駄な情報がない）
- [ ] Supporting the presenter's ideas（話の内容に合う適切なものとなっている）
- [ ] Not using too many graphics（スライド内に図やグラフが多すぎない）
- [ ] Using clear graphics（図、写真、絵が見やすい）

▼ **Content**
- [ ] Full and rich development of content（内容が充実している）
- [ ] Focused and brief message（内容がテーマに沿っており、簡潔にまとめられている）
- [ ] Sufficient explanation and supporting information（テーマの支持情報が充分にある）
- [ ] Clearly stated positions（筆者の視点が明らか）
- [ ] Easy to follow（内容が理解しやすい）
- [ ] Not too long or too short（長すぎず、短すぎない）
- [ ] Containing relevant information（無駄な情報がない）

Presentation Rubric

Presenter's Name [   ]

	Poor = 1	Adequate = 2	Good = 3	Excellent = 4
Organization	No clear structure (introduction, body, conclusion); ideas are ordered illogically.	Somewhat unclear structure (introduction, body, conclusion); ideas are sometimes illogically ordered.	Somewhat clear structure (introduction, body, conclusion); ideas are mostly logically ordered.	Very clear structure (introduction, body, conclusion); ideas are always logically ordered.
Language	Explanation is often difficult to understand. Many spelling and punctuation errors.	Explanation is sometimes difficult to understand. Some spelling and punctuation errors.	Explanation is usually easy to understand. Few spelling and punctuation errors.	Explanation is almost always easy to understand. Almost no spelling or punctuation errors.
Visual Aids	Design of visual aids often makes presentation hard to follow.	Design of visual aids sometimes makes presentation hard to follow.	Design of visual aids usually makes presentation easy to follow.	Design of visual aids always makes presentation easy to follow.
Presentation Skills	Little or no eye contact; unclear, monotone voice; negative body language.	Inconsistent eye contact; somewhat unclear, monotone voice; neutral body language.	Somewhat consistent eye contact; clear voice with some intonation and stress; somewhat positive body language.	Very consistent eye contact; clear voice with natural intonation and stress; positive body language.

Student ID [   ] Name [   ]

3-Point Academic Writing:
Organization, Content, Language
3つの要素で学ぶアカデミック・ライティングの基本

2019年1月20日　初版第1刷発行
2024年2月20日　初版第6刷発行

著者　深 山 晶 子
　　　幸 重 美津子
　　　尾 鍋 智 子
　　　村 尾 純 子
　　　Ashley Moore

発行者　福 岡 正 人
発行所　株式会社　金 星 堂

（〒101-0051）東京都千代田区神田神保町 3-21
　　　Tel　（03）3263-3828（営業部）
　　　　　　（03）3263-3997（編集部）
　　　Fax　（03）3263-0716
　　　https://www.kinsei-do.co.jp

編集担当　松本 明子　　　　Printed in Japan
印刷所・製本所／倉敷印刷株式会社
本書の無断複製・複写は著作権法上での例外を除き禁じられています。
本書を代行業者等の第三者に依頼してスキャンやデジタル化することは、
たとえ個人や家庭内での利用であっても認められておりません。
落丁・乱丁本はお取り替えいたします。

ISBN978-4-7647-4087-7　C1082